LET'S WORRY ABOUT EVERYTHING

Cassie Shea

*I've worried about everything so you don't have to...
You're welcome.*

The Awakened Press
www.theawakenedpress.com

For information about special discounts for bulk purchases, please
contact The Awakened Press at books@theawakenedpress.com.

The Awakened Press can bring authors to your live event. For more
information or to book an event contact
books@theawakenedpress.com or visit our website at
www.theawakenedpress.com.

Cover and book design by Kurt A. Dierking II

Printed in the United States of America
First The Awakened Press trade paperback edition

ISBN: 979-8-9860377-8-3

LET'S WORRY ABOUT EVERYTHING

Cassie Shea

*I've worried about everything so you don't have to...
You're welcome.*

The Awakened Press

To Mom for teaching me

To Dad for feeding me

To my brother for growing with me

To my soulmates for finding me

To the readers for laughing with me

Contents

The World's Most Worried Toddler

Cassie has always loved words. As a little girl, she would use big words in her everyday conversations. I remember a visit to my folk's house once, and my father was setting up a blow-up pool for Cassie. She was about eighteen months old. When she saw it, she said, "Oh, Papa, that pool is enormous!" We were all so surprised that a word like that would come out of such a little mouth!

I loved talking with her and reading books together out loud. I would read non-picture books and tell Cassie at an early age to make the pictures in her head to go along with the story. I think this was when she first fell in love with writing stories for herself.

Cassie wanted to learn to read and write at three years old. Little did I know that this would be her destiny. As I homeschooled both of my children through the years, it became evident to me that Cassie needed further instruction in writing than what I could give her. Fortunately, our homeschooling group included some moms whose specialty was writing. With their tutelage, Cassie had a great beginning as an author, thanks to these lovely ladies who invested so much into her wordy craft.

Now, you may be wondering where the "worrying" part comes in. Well, Cassie comes by this quite naturally because it is in her genes. Her paternal great-grandma and maternal great-granddad were both "great" worriers! Cassie's dad has told her many times that her Great-Grandma Anne (pronounced "Annie") was called Anxious Annie because she worried about all sorts of things. As for my granddad—well, I can't remember a time when Llewellyn wasn't worrying about something—from when dinner was going to be prepared, to who would win the baseball game, or when his oldest daughter would arrive home.

This brings to mind the first time I realized that Cassie had acquired the "worrying gene." She was about two and a half years old and had just been potty trained. She very proudly flushed the toilet herself but then a terrible thing happened... The toilet backed up and overflowed, and Cassie started to cry, worrying that the entire city was going to flood! It took me quite a while to calm her down and assure her that no flood would occur in our beloved hometown.

As Cassie grew, she loved being a part of everything. With that came more to worry about! Much time was spent counseling her to not worry about what people thought of her, or whether she had the appropriate fashionable outfit to wear. She would worry if she was going to get invited to certain functions even though she was too young to go, anyway. She worried if we would still love her if she became physically deformed somehow. She also worried about how she would provide for herself, buy her first car, and buy a home. All this worrying came before she was even a teenager! Sometimes I asked her if she was reading too many books and told her just to relax and go play outside.

The day finally came when Cassie confided she had started writing her first book. She and I had taken my mom out to lunch, and afterward we were all sitting down, having a cappuccino in an outdoor plaza. Cassie asked me if I would like to preview it. I was so excited to take a peek at what she was working on. I started reading her manuscript out loud to my mom. Soon into it, I was laughing so hard that my mom could not understand a word I was saying.

From that moment onward, I encouraged Cassie to get this book written! I love to laugh, and I think the world needs more levity. I am honored that Cassie would ask me to write this foreword and I hope you enjoy and laugh throughout the pages.

More than anything, I hope this book helps all the worriers out there know there is someone who has worried about everything, so you don't have to.

Lovingly, Cassie's Devoted Mom,
Cherie Shea

Worry: A Lifetime Achievement Award

Instead of spending an evening celebrating celebrities at an awards show, I always wondered what it would be like to celebrate real people living their real lives.

If there was such a thing as an awards program in a toasty, roasty, hilarious fashion for everyday citizens, the evening of extraordinary elegance I would try to sweep is the *Worry Awards*.

It would go something like this... Your family and friends would nominate you for an award like, "Most Worried about Their Wardrobe," "Most Worried about Facial Wrinkles," "Most Worried about Falling Off a Horse While Riding Bareback," "Most Worried about What They're Eating Next," "Most Worried about Future Travel Plans Going Wrong," "Most Worried about an Imbalanced 401(k) Portfolio," "Most Worried about Having Kids with the Wrong Person," and then you'd have contestants explain why they're worried. They'd out-worry each other. Then, we could all collectively vote on which person is most worried. And, as a viewer, you'd feel a sense of relief that you are not the only person who is worried about...everything.

Illustriously, the award I would probably win is, "Most Worried About Worrying." I worry about how I worry, when I worry, why I worry, and how much I worry. I worry about telling people about my worries. Will it be too much? Will they worry about me worrying?

Many, many people have told me simply, "*Don't worry.*" This has never helped me. Has it ever helped anyone? I doubt it. Someone telling a professional worrier not to worry is definitely the same person who doesn't pull through to the gasoline pump when there is a spot open ahead of them and instead blocks the entire lane. They're probably the type of person who takes ten minutes to order in a drive-through line when there are only three items on the menu. Some people just aren't worried enough, in my opinion.

Doctors have told me not to worry. That's pretty suspicious, if you ask me. When I was eighteen years old, a sophomore in college, I was medically informed that the "tummy ache" I was experiencing was clinically known as pre-ulcers. The doctor told me I should relax more and worry less. I picked up another major and a minor just to show him otherwise. I went from working two part-time jobs to four part-time jobs. I doubled my output and doubled the fun! What did he know about me from a thirty-second interaction about how much pain I was in, on a scale of one to ten?

I've spent my whole life worrying. I feel that worrying is one of my distinct, crowning achievements. I come from a long line of worry warriors; my Irish great-grandma was fondly known as "Anxious Annie." She drank a shot of whiskey, nightly, for medicinal reasons. Those are my reasons, too, when I consume Jameson.

I can see myself having one too many drinks and boasting at a cocktail party that my worry is my badge of honor. It's what sets me apart. "It's what I've done more frequently and better than you," I'd say while guzzling bourbon. And then I'd worry about what people think of my drinking habits, since ladies don't typically imbibe bourbon.

Wait, did you think I was going to say I was worried about my drinking? Hardly! I'm pretending to be a writer, and writers tend to consume alcohol.

Whenever I run out of things to worry about, that worries me the most. More than once, I've told my mom, dad, brother, favorite aunt, extended family, best friends, mediocre friends, auxiliary friends, ex-boyfriends, ex-husbands, massage therapists, meditation teachers, customer service representatives while on a long hold, random people I met online, and even strangers at the grocery store that if I'm not worried, I'm most likely dead.

So many painstaking hours have been spent worrying about this worry. I've paid others to worry about my worry for me (like therapists). I've paid others to tell me how to stop worrying (like coaches). I've tried channeling my worry in other directions (like hobbies). I've even paused my worrying, albeit briefly, and tried to take a break (like a vacation). I don't like the phrase "respite from worry," as it implies that I'm somehow done with worrying, and now I feel queasy.

I've also spent an inordinate amount of money to cure my worry (more like *worries*). Money spent on things like self-help books, self-help online courses, therapy, doctors' visits, massages, facials, trips to the steam room, expensive vacations, books to distract me, show streaming subscriptions, a better apartment, moving in general, day trips, brunch, better liquor, meditation classes, sound baths, light shows, pet rocks, candles, new bedding, a wardrobe change... I mean, the list is long.

I'm in no way alone in this worry. I don't live on a worry island. I know many folks in America are consumed with Generalized Anxiety Disorder (GAD), which saw a spike in over 6.8 million cases during the year of 2020 (the most dumpster-fire year in our collective history, anthropologically speaking). That's over 3% of the American population. And yes, excessive, but in general, anxiety is diagnosable. It's real, people. I'm not self-diagnosing, for reference. I'm just bringing your attention to a thing that exists, in case you thought, *Wow, she didn't worry about this.* I did. I want you to know I'm worry-credible.

GSD appears in The Diagnostic and Statistical Manual of Mental Disorders (DSM). I know what the DSM is, and I know how "they" use it. I worry that I know too much. I know we're all in the DSM. I think there's a small asterisk by the word "worry" that has my initials, date of birth, and perhaps my mother's maiden name in case you misplace any of my aliases. I could be a case study. Then I'd have to volunteer to talk to people, which would take time away from my reading or writing about worry, so this is probably not going to happen anytime soon. Or at least before my eyesight runs out.

Here's the thing. I've spent over 10,000 hours worrying for you, becoming a deep and wide expert on worry (as 10,000 hours is the approximate amount of time it takes one human to become an expert on something, or at least I read that once, somewhere). And maybe you can live vicariously through my worry to ease your own. Or, perhaps you can live through my worry and simply laugh at me. I'm very much resigned to worrying. I'm also hoping that either way, you'll find something meaningful, heartfelt, and true in here. And if the wiles of fate smile upon me, I'd consider myself wildly fortunate if I made you laugh out loud.

I want to discuss the deep things I truly worry about with a cathartic dose of comedy, mostly so these stories are palatable to us both. And so that my mom doesn't worry too much about me after reading my worries. I have to consider the butterfly effect, here. I hope you find a way to laugh *at me.* I'm volunteering for this. And perhaps you'll be able to ease a bit of your own worry by feeling less isolated, less neurotic (I take the trophy), and less serious.

I mean, with all seriousness, you gotta lighten up if you want to read this book to the end. I can't take your dour look while you're padding through the murky waters of all my deep, dark secrets and laughing at me behind my back.

You don't always find your path in life by looking for it straight on. Sometimes, your path finds you. When I decided to finally embrace my unique gift—which is, well, worrying about everything—I realized I wasn't really all that alone. Other people have worries, too. Delightfully, I discovered over time that if I made jokes about what I was worried about, no one could make fun of me, because I was already fun.

And so, without further adieu, let's proceed to worry about everything. Together.

Chapter 1

Let's Worry about our Worst Fears

I don't know your worst fears. But I'll tell you all of mine (at least, the ones I can recall) in case it helps you worry about your fears a little bit less.

Worrying about my worries might just add worry to your already full plate. You might discover something new to worry about, or realize there are far weirder worries out there than your own.

I'll give you a lens into my very worst fears. You're welcome.

Death by Cranberry Juice

If I could go back in time and play a character on *Seinfeld*, I would be akin to Jerry's ex-girlfriend, "The Sipper." I don't sip delicately. I don't sip quietly. Like the lady whose man hands were inescapably obvious, you simply cannot mistake my horrible, outrageous, loud gulping.

And when I want to indulge in my thunderous quaffing, my drink of choice is cranberry juice. Not the sugar-coated apple or raspberry infused cranberry cocktail. I like the zero sugar added, 100% straight, bitter, garnet-red, unadulterated juice. I love it so much that every time I go to drink it, I end up wheezing and inhaling and coughing until I can no longer drink in my standard, just-slightly-over-the-top-annoyingly-loud way.

I love it so much, it's like I feel I need to take it all in at once, before it disappears. There's never been a run on 100%, no-sugar-added cranberry juice of late, but you never know when it might happen.

I never feared cranberry juice until the other night. I woke up, desperately thirsty, and headed to the kitchen for a calming liquid concoction. I mixed LaCroix—bourgeois-flavored sparkling water—with cranberry juice. As the apple was to Eve—tantalizing, forbidden, luscious, and irresistible—so was this nefarious nectar. I could not be satiated with one sip! *I must consume and destroy!* It was like all of my world domination feelings were thrown at one cup.

In my half-awake state that night, I forgot to pretend to sip daintily and proceeded to swig down the cranberry juice. It was the middle of the night. I was thirsty. Then I was basically half-dead, choking down cranberry juice, trying to catch my breath, wondering if my end was looming before me in the dark hours of my now sleepless night.

Alas. I now eyeball the cranberry juice in my fridge with an air of suspicion. What was once such a close friend could be the dagger in my throat on my next insomniac adventure!

Accidentally Singing during a Live Performance

Whether it's seeing Plácedo Domingo sing *Macbeth*, or the local high school theater group perform *Grease*, I am paranoid I will break into song during a live performance. I do know a few Italian arias, but don't worry, I didn't memorize *Macbeth* before seeing it. I do, however, know every line of music in the theatrical or cinema version of *Grease*.

I don't know where it started or how it happened. There's no backstory to this plot. Whenever I see a live musical performance, my heart starts beating really hard and I get clammy hands. I start to feel dizzy. Once, when reviewing my ticket stub, I knew rationally that I paid a lot of money to be there. Even though I was likely on a date, I'm a recovering egalitarian feminist who (falsely) believed I should always pay my way. Hooey. Hoobastank. Hell's bells. I was hoodwinked into believing it was powerful to show I could pay my own way. Now I just save myself the trouble; I don't date at all, and stay home drinking wine in my pajamas and eating pasta in bed. *What are your plans this Friday, Cassie? Pasta and wine in bed.* This answer will likely never change. Even if I do other activities, I'll probably still tell you I'm drinking wine and eating pasta in bed because this is clearly a good life choice and it keeps me out of trouble.

It's showtime. I clasp my hands when the curtain is called, which most people would think is in anticipation or elation at the production. Really, it's a signal to my body NOT to sing.

Sometimes I sit on my hands and lean forward. Other audience members who are likewise enraptured might note my posture and think, wow, she loves it. She's really leaning in. Wait, I forgot mostly everyone is a self-obsessed narcissist. You could probably run around naked in a theater and no one would notice you. Don't worry, I haven't tried this yet in the name of research, or otherwise. This thought came to me in 2020 when everything was already cancelled.

I'm not sure where this worry originated. But whenever I start to hum along with the show, I take a breath, clamp my body into submission, and grit and bear the rest of the performance. I worry if I'll get my money's worth as I attempt to enjoy the performance, whilst holding my breath and sitting on my hands. Usually, at this point, I haven't passed out yet. Now that I mention it, that gives me something new to worry about, too. Meanwhile, the show does go on, as they say.

Driving into a Concrete Wall

I'm not the worst driver I've ever met. I would not go as far as to say I'm the greatest driver, either. I can tell you that I gave up a lot of my bad habits. I don't text and drive anymore (I almost crashed a small handful of times). I also don't eat and drive (I spilled on myself quite often before giving this one up). I don't sip coffee and drive (one stained white dress skirt and one very burned leg were enough to swear me off this merry-go-round). I try not to change musical stations on the radio unless I'm at a stoplight (swerving and tuning don't jive for me). I try to put my directions into Google Maps before I leave for my destination (I have a bad sense of direction, so this is mostly self-preservation, and finally admitting my flaws to myself out loud). I don't do my makeup while driving (mostly because I can poke my eye with the mascara wand while standing still, so I'm nervous what would happen if I were in motion). And, I avoid yelling at Siri in traffic lest someone perceives it as road rage and engages in unfriendly behavior with myself and my car, which was affectionately known as Grandma (thus far, I have not been embroiled in a road rage scheme with anyone).

I drive like a grandma, mostly. I named my car Grandma. I listen to the radio like I am a grandma. My car was so old there was no Bluetooth, Pandora input or whatever the kids use these days. I have strategically limited my distractions and improved my car habits immensely, thanks to a father who is defensive driving certified. I might be certifiable.

To make commuting more bearable, I wonder what it would look like to have a dating app match people up based on their routes to work. A suggested Starbucks date spot on the app would come with a two-for-one latte coupon. Naturally, this is how I would monetize: selling location-specific advertising space. I came up with this idea in 2020, when everyone went remote and no one commuted anywhere anymore, unless it was from their bed to the kitchen to refill their Goldfish cracker bowl and get a new can of sparkling water (please tell me other sane-ish adults still eat fishy crackers, too).

My biggest fear with driving is that I will crash into the concrete divider. The divider would sneak out of nowhere, obviously. It could be in a construction area. Or on the freeway. I wouldn't crash because I'm texting, eating, putting on mascara, or doing some externally distracting task. The thing that would sink me is my brain. I'm normally so deep in thought or I'm singing the *Grease* soundtrack at the top of my lungs, I worry I'll forget I'm driving at all. Sometimes I do forget. Don't tell my dad.

It's been a distinct, crowning achievement of mine to memorize each line of the *Grease* soundtrack. This endeavor seemed like an apt use of my fourteen years of sitting in Los Angeles traffic day in and day out. You have to find ways of entertaining yourself that are legal and not accident-inducing. This rule, coincidentally, ruled out stock trading on your phone, which the cop might misconstrue as "texting."

If I were a better person, I could have learned stuff on podcasts or books online. But I thought it would make more sense to listen to 1970s musicals on repeat. That's kinda how I am in my natural environment: making quality decisions, on repeat. Now you know.

Being an Angeleno for over a decade, I can tell you that we all lived on the road. You slept somewhere. But you lived your life— the waking hours between dawn and dusk—as a captive prisoner to the freeways. Freedom ain't free.

Conscious commuters, as opposed to the comatose ones, learn each peak and plummet of the road until you feel the road under your car carving out a story, like someone might master reading Braille. I knew each pothole, turn, caveat, and crusty area on my daily commute. I feared the new distractions, and the construction zones, which were the dark, insidious, unexpected, chaotic matter on my otherwise calm and collected route. I worried I would run into a new divider and median since it wasn't there the last 467 times I did the exact same drive, in the exact same traffic, with the exact same person next to me in the exact same beat-up Mazda.

Everything Goes Wrong during Your Own Live Performance

Performing was a major part of my life growing up. And because I worried about everything going wrong, and mostly everything did, I stopped this particular form of public torture at the tender age of sixteen.

I worried about falling down on stage, in a non-metaphorical way. Magically, this came true. Perhaps there is something to this idea of a law of attraction—what you think becomes reality. I'm not sure how many times I fell down, which gives you an indicator I was a repeat offender. The most memorable tumble was in my early teenage years, just after I "blossomed" in the chest region and graduated into a real bra. I was wearing a pencil skirt and heels, which is a lot to ask of someone with a newly minted woman body to manage. I stumbled on the stairs, and worried my shirt would flash everyone. The thing is, I suppose it's better to flash an audience while wearing a bra versus not having a bra on. Of course, I was too mortified to consider this at the time, so I turned beet red and soldiered on with my showtunes.

One of my piano teachers, bless her, had the audacity to imagine I could be a real contender in the area of piano performances. I started lessons around age ten, which is approximately eleven years too late to become a truly great pianist. She decided that to increase my moxie and get me out of my comfort zone, I would play the piano without having my notes in front of me. Ensconced in an intimate, candle-lit circular chapel, I held the rapt attention of my audience. The cylindrical design had the worrisome architecture, allowing your entire audience to peer, ardently, into your tender teenage face while you played the piano.

I forgot every single note. My mind went blank. I didn't have time to worry about this at the moment of impact because I was enraptured at staring at my hands over the black-and-white keys and remembering absolutely nothing. No thoughts. No notes. No motion. I was suspended in space and time, alert of how painstakingly inert my life had become. People pay a lot of money to learn how to clear their head through meditation. You could more simply just induce anxiety in front of a live audience and generate the same result of a blank brain. Truthfully, I am not even sure if I completed my performance or not. I blacked it out. I blacked out then and wiped the memory from my hard drive because I'm an automaton like that when it comes to embarrassing emotions. It was horrifying. My piano teacher moved away right in the middle of teaching me Beethoven's *Moonlight Sonata*. I think she hated me, specifically, and thus ran away to some other part of the country to start a fresh life.

Rounding out my performance training, I took vocal lessons for seven years. I only tap danced for a few months. It was hard to do both at one time. Speaking of my singing career for just a moment: my singing teacher coached some people who are now YouTube stars and worth upwards of two million dollars. Retrospectively,

I want a refund. I clearly did not monetize myself well enough. And I blame my singing teacher for not believing in me.

First off, my professional jazz musician and perfectly lovely blonde singing coach had perfect pitch, which is suspect enough if you ask me. Secondly, when I was entering a statewide singing competition, we proceeded to select my music. I wanted to perform something big and bold because I was sixteen by this point and felt I had nothing to lose. Life hadn't beaten me down yet. This was the phase where I would often sing "On My Own" from *Les Misérables* to express my teenage angst, during the same time other folks were learning HTML to code their Myspace.

I found the song that would redeem my performing career. It would showcase my range. It would make me a suitable star, and really let me embrace a fuller, bolder, bigger style (I kind of pitched myself like a quality red wine). The song? "Habanera." My teacher, however, did not think I was dramatic enough to sing *Carmen*. *Not dramatic enough.* She's the only person who has ever said this to me. I'm not holding a grudge, per se, but I think she did not artfully consider my capacity for hyperbole and hysterics. If only she could have channeled me better, I might have been a contender.

I switched to singing to put my embarrassing, dying-on-the-vine piano career behind me forever. At sixteen, I was used to making the tough calls. "This department has been discontinued," I told myself when a change was needed. Clear of vision, I was. This hardened me for a future career in Human Resources, and the practice came in handy so I could fire a lot of people. I thought I had made it to an easy street after a lifetime of shower singing and car karaoke. What I didn't realize I should have worried about was having your voice crack in the middle of the performance. It's hard to find a script that details what to do when you biff a note so badly it could puncture crystal glassware. The only reasonable thing to do is smile and keep going. I worried that people would call me a quitter if I ran off stage and cried, so I saved that for the private after-party, also known as the pity party of one.

Another health hazard in the sport of singing is locking one's knees. I've regaled you with tales of folly and falling, but standing up and standing still was also really hard for me. I'm not sure if anyone has invented a real, happy medium here. I worried about tumbling over, so I would lock my knees because they shook like a palm tree bending in a hurricane. *Grit and bear it. Lock the jaw. Just get through this awful experience called a "live performance."*

I think the kindest thing to do with kids who have stage fright might be to just let them stay home. In my wonderful, serene, suburban house, I safely listened to every single line of music ever released by Celine Dion, beat my chest, and was assured my heart would go on. Instead, my parents paid ludicrous amounts of money for me to feel tortured. And for what? Just to win a couple of singing competitions? I never even got to audition for *American Idol*. When I worry it might be too late, I realize *American Idol* just signed on for season number seventeen million, and so maybe there's hope for me yet.

Finally, if everything in the whole entire performance goes wrong, there's still one last thing to worry about: the receiving line. People who donated their genetics to your biology—and apparently want to see you flourish as a human being—have the audacity to wish to speak to you. For some unknown reason, they want to tell you afterward what a good job you have done. I wonder if they're somehow paid to say this? Because of the worry-inducing rigamarole I have endured, I shouldn't have been shaking anyone's hand. From the falling to the clanking of my knees to the cracking of my voice, my body hated performing so much, my palms were clammy. I couldn't shake anyone's hand because my hands were as moist as a luscious cake.

Falling Off a Rooftop Bar

It seems like a notoriously bad idea to allow people to become inebriated at heights. How ungrounding. The only veil concealing me from crawling to my death at a rooftop bar is a cagey glass structure. It looks nice. It looks serene. But looks can be deceiving. I could easily become drunk and bet someone I could crawl over it. I wouldn't. But I could. And knowing I have had this thought, who else has shared it? Secretly, we all want to defy death in the name of public intoxication. Isn't that why karaoke bars even exist? It certainly is what keeps 24-hour pancake houses in business past midnight.

My deepest fear with rooftop bars is that I will get carried away in conversation and carried into the clouds. I'm not sure this would be the worst way to die. I might be so high (literally, not figuratively) and so happy (alcohol, for once, would capitulate me into euphoria; I've heard this is possible), that I don't notice my own imminent demise. Generally, that's how I want to go. Happy. I wonder how many factors of universal laws have to be at play for this possibility to become a reality.

Missing the Turn

One of my favorite poems is about two roads diverging into a wood. You know it, I'm sure. You're a literate person and all (I'm giving you that one on the house). If on the off chance you don't know, or you're drinking, it goes like this: There are two paths. How tidy and binary. The paths diverge. You can only walk one path. And the path the author chooses is the path less traveled.

I happen to really like paved paths. If I can find a hiking trail with a paved path, I'm more likely to exercise there because it seems less likely a Ted Bundy type would be on such a well-developed, well-trafficked road. On the opposing view, serial killers might prefer paved paths because there are less footprints. Perhaps this gives them easier access to stash the body in the truck. And, my friends, this is why I exercise on my driveway. Safely at home. Away from nature. Away from the type of serial killers who would frequent asphalt-laden hiking routes.

The paths that are less traveled diverging into unknown woods frankly scare the hell out of me. I don't have a machete. I can't whack bushes. I can't start a fire from scratch. And I can't read a compass. Nor a map. In fact, one of my very first inquisitions on a casual first date is, "How do you rate your navigation skills?" I like to throw softball questions out. But, I also really need to know, because I'm the kind of person who can get lost in Costco.

My eternal question about this two-path poem, and one I've never gotten a straight answer to, is this: isn't there a certain kind of romance to a well-oiled, well-paved, well-known path? No one ever talks about the sexy benefits to simply doing things that work—like saving money and capitalizing on compound interest. I mean, I can't tell you this story personally because I've drained my retirement 401(k) a couple times, both of which had to do with divorce-related expenses. If you ever hear of a story where everything just works out peachy keen for someone following sage, time-old advice in a meandering, nice fashion on a paved pathway, well, I'd love to interview them personally.

There's a suspicious component of timing and synchronicity in this whole turn theory, here. Something that wreaks of luck, which is a bit hard to pin down and define. What if I'm at the right place, at the right time, with the right people, and I miss the "turn" that changes my life? I wrote this sentence just after a lovely lunch and now I feel nauseous. Worrying about everything for you, dear reader, is a precious pledge and I will pursue it with dignity. I am not claiming I might not make myself violently ill in the process; I'm nothing but a method actor dedicated to going all the way on your behalf.

Another component of missing this metaphorical turn is listening to life advice. What if you get the right life advice from the wrong person? What if you get the wrong life advice from the right person? What if people aren't as right or wrong as *they* think they are? What if people aren't as right or wrong as *you* think they are? What if you listen to other people's advice at the expense of your own longings? What if you don't listen to someone's advice because you're in a state of longing? What if your intuition goes on a vacation and forgets to log in for a meeting? What if you tried to outsource your intuition to a psychic and they ate the wrong thing at lunch and saw the wrong timeline?

Advice is such a sticky business. That's why I prefer coaching. Getting paid to ask people questions is a helluva lot better than telling them what to do. If you tell them what to do, they'll likely ask you for a refund. Looking at my life, I'd definitely ask for a refund on a couple of experiences. Speaking of which, if that's available, do email me. Yes, I still use email.

Speaking of missing the turn, in a strictly non-metaphorical way now, this harkens back to my fear of winding mountain road driving. I'll come out and say it plain and clear: I trust other people to drive mountain roads more than I trust myself. I'll vet the driver. They need a valid license, current registration, and a good deal on auto insurance (I can't be seen driving around with people who pay 15% more).

The thing with me and windy driving could be summarized this way: I honestly don't trust myself to stick my eyes where I should. Cars seem to drift in the direction of our attention. Perhaps they are not unlike thoughts manifesting into ever-present, material realities. The thing is, I always want to look over the cliff's edge as a way of proclaiming I'm not *really* that afraid of heights. Now, if I'm driving, that means my car is perpetually turned toward the cliff. And everyone, even me, knows that over-correction is a sure-fire way to sudden death.

So, there you have it. Attempting to conquer my fears could lead to a sudden, specific, seemingly irreversible catastrophe, otherwise known as death. And I think you're lying if you tell me, "Just face your fears, it'll all work out fine." Because this much I do know: death, like Las Vegas, offers no refunds.

Getting Robbed at the Beach

Of all the places to get your stuff stolen, the worst location would be the place where you're (mostly) publicly nude. Stating the obvious, it's nearly impossible to chase someone down at the beach due to the sand. It's either sticky and soggy, or lusciously warm and inviting for sunbathing, both of which make it less than ideal for kerfuffles and confrontations with lawlessness. Perhaps there is a universal law that states that the location in which you enjoy maximum relaxation can, by the transitive property of letting your guard down and becoming too happy, become your deadliest downfall if you need to mount a quick affront to a perpetrator. The solution is to become slightly less happy, and stay outside of sun-drenched coastlines, I'm sure.

Less obvious but equally true, and perhaps Cassie's survival guide lesson one: no one cares to help. I don't stop and ask, "Hey, how are you?" when I see people who look mildly distressed or unnerved. It's also just my least favorite question on the planet.

"How are you?" What a banal, uninspired idea for a sentence. If someone asks me, "Hey, how are you?" there's a high likelihood I will say something like, "Doing well, just got home from my spacecraft mission in the Minar region and I'm planning my next asteroid mining adventure into the Andromeda Galaxy." Chances are, they didn't ask because they want to hear my real answer, so I might as well make something up. I'm a writer, after all.

If there is an actual, honest-to-goodness, real emergency, I would simply call 911. I would not personally stop to help. You probably worry I've lost my moral compass, which is one thing I don't worry about 90% of the time. I save that for only a 10% worry occupation slot. See, the thing is, I'm 5'2.5". I'm not a trained Krav Maga warrior or a prime time cage fighter, so I'm pretty useless in a physical battle. In a verbal altercation, I could likely hold my own, but I prefer long, windy, psychological battles to steam-engine yelling brawls. None of this makes me a good candidate to help a bystander in distress, or really solve my worry about beach thievery.

There's a lot of other mishaps that could occur during this potential robbery in progress, which include Houdini-level escapes. The perp can disappear into the crowd. Or, if I'm swimming whilst watching the heist, I could disappear into the ocean. Having any altercations with life-threatening water next to you also ratchets up the ante on this fear. What if the tide comes in suddenly? What if the tide goes out suddenly and the beach disappears while I'm getting robbed? Then you're getting robbed while the literal ground underneath you erodes and disappears.

The only rational way I've thought to somewhat reduce this worry is to get a fanny pack, which worries me about my level of comfort with becoming someone who has gotten a fanny pack. So, the only sane thing I've come up with is to hide my fanny pack in a blanket and hide the blanket somewhere, which leaves me exposed in the process of tearing off clothes and fanny packs and re-bundling everything while looking over my shoulder for potential beach perps.

Or, I walk up to a kindly group of mothers and proclaim I'm single and my dad wants me to be safe "out here." I wait for them to nod knowingly, and proceed to ask, "Would you please watch my stuff as I jump in the ocean?" Since I still look relatively young, whatever that means, usually they say yes.

So my new theory is that moms can be the best bodyguards, or they could start a sting operation for pickpocketing fanny packs without worriers ever suspecting them.

Flossing with Fishbones

The first time I ate Korean food, I was twenty-six. This fact is irrelevant to the story, but I'm the writer here, after all, not you. Anyway, I sat down, and ordered soon tofu with dumplings. It couldn't have come sooner. I felt like I ate an entire meal before I got my not-so-soon tofu.

Korean main dishes are only enjoyed after a buffet of banchan. The direct translation of banchan is "side dishes," but I think this fails to convey the excitement of an array of tiny, delicate dishes dancing with flavors and substances of ingredients you cannot name, pronounce, or recognize from the standard American diet. There were no menu details, and I was frankly afraid to ask for more information.

One of my biggest worries about food is that I won't know what I'm eating when I eat it. I worry I will eat something unfamiliar; I won't know what it is and like it. Or, I might know what it is and then in knowing, dislike it, thus ruining my fun. As it turned out, I regrettably discovered what my favorite banchan was: fishcakes and pickled squid. I hate squid on a normal day, but pickle it? Picked, it tickled my fancy. It's mostly better not to ask what a dish is composed of, thus running the element of surprise, and I resumed shoveling it into my mouth with chopsticks.

I also learned if you are going to ask for seconds at a Korean establishment, you better be sure as hell you can finish it. Leaving food on your plate is such a disgrace that some restaurants will actually charge you for not finishing your food. Once, I had to hide my food at the bottom of the broth and just say I couldn't finish my soup. I was about to ask if I could mail it off to a starving orphan in North Korea, but somehow I figured that joke would get me banned for life. I've seen it happen to other patrons. "You're banned for life," they were told. Korean restaurateurs really employ their right to refuse service to anyone. I couldn't abide with having to learn how to pickle my own squid.

Dried mackerel is the banchan that no self-respecting human under age sixty-five eats anymore. Imagine a fish fried in a frier, head on, bones in, eyes looking right at you. The fish is tiny, about the size of a large dinner roll. And your objective? To pluck the once fried, now dried, fishy meat off the bone without flossing your teeth with the aforementioned bones. The bones are so microscopic that you need a magnifying glass to discern flesh from bone. Like a vulture, or a surgeon, I would go in with my chopstick implements and peel away the skin delicately, and retrieve one millimeter bite at a time. When I looked around to refocus my eyes away from the fineness of this task, I realized I was one of the only youthful people attempting this feat in the restaurant. I got curious nods and glances. I had a toothy grin on my face. Likely, full of fishbones.

I didn't know to worry about bones becoming flossing implements until I tried to eat the mackerel. I've also choked on these feather-thin bones, too. Essentially, it's a hazard to my health to access what might amount, in total, to one measly mouthful. I wonder, truthfully, if I just succumbed to the flossing process, would this replace my need for calcium supplements? Do fishbones contain enough calcium and collagen to be the secret fountain of youth? Speaking of the unending fountain of youth...

Skincare and Aging

In my early twenties, I read that your skin starts to age rapidly at age twenty-nine. When I turned twenty-eight, I knew it was all downhill from there. I fortified my twenty-ninth birthday with expensive face sunscreen, first. Second, I started a rapid acquisition of serums, oils, potions, and lotions that I had no idea what they did or how they worked together. Ever since, I have made it my mission to get semi-regular facials, massage my skin, rub oil on me like I'm a roasted duck, and purchase skincare with promising results.

Most of the skincare in America doesn't interest me. It feels fad-ish or fake, somehow. Every time I go abroad, I make it my express mission to purchase eye cream in a foreign country. The more expensive, the better. The way I figure it, perhaps, is that regulations are different in other countries and they can pad their ageless solutions with ingredients that are illegal in America. Maybe my eye serum contains stem cells. Maybe it contains LSD. Maybe it contains stardust. Maybe it contains uranium. I don't trust it when it says 24-karat gold; I'm not that naïve (nor rich). Doesn't really matter that I can't read the label, and no, I don't bother to translate it. Hope springs eternal.

I've amassed around seventy-five skincare products for my anti-aging rotation. My friends who are the same age, and similarly concerned with defying the gravitational pull of the suffrage of sag, ask, "What do you do to your face?" It's an interesting question. Basically, I slap on a bunch of things I find abroad and hope for the best.

I don't have a routine.

I don't have a rhythm.

There is no reasonable process to it.

I put this on and that on. And then add some things. And slap it. I mean, really slap it in, because one facialist told me to get skincare to perform, you must rub vigorously. It's like skincare with sound effects. *Ping! Pow! Bam!* I press eye cream into my one forehead wrinkle because I figure I should use the most expensive item on the sole, deep-divot wrinkle. At around thirty-something, I have just one wrinkle so far and my brother says it's because I look at other people like they are "dumb" (his words). Apparently, if I stopped judging people, I would be wrinkle-free. Something to marinate on. (In my defense, have you met people? They're the worst.)

I use my ring finger to apply the eye serum because that's the only area that you're really, really not supposed to slap and pull. My emotions do that just fine when I cry my eyes out, anyway. I call it a proprietary, salinity stream bath when that happens. Whenever someone asks me, "Why are you crying?" from now on I just respond that it's part of the anti-aging routine I have. Better out than in.

I have it on a to-tackle-someday list to learn proper facial massage to simulate a facelift. It's also a great way to reduce jaw tension. I never worry, of late, if I have a locked jaw or not when I sit in front of the mirror and say "ahhhhhhh" while moving my jaw and skin around. Because things are moving, and motion is medicine, I'm hoping that somehow it makes me look twenty-nine for at least a few more years. Just kidding, I never go outside, so no one knows what I look like, anyway.

"You're only thirty," my friends would say. "What's the point of eye cream? I don't see it making a heap of difference." I nod. Silently, I know the truth: it's like compound interest. The results will be there, in twenty-something years. I'm banking on it. At this very moment, I have Korean, Indian, French, English, and American varieties of eye creams, specifically.

"Aren't you concerned that you don't have a process? How do you know what to put on first? How do you know how the products interact with each other? What if you're allergic to an ingredient from your travel-collected creams?" These are all good things to worry about, I'll give it to you. But the way I've found to resolve some worries, or at least subside them, is to have a meta-worry. A trump card worry. A worry that blows all other worries away. And my meta-face-worry is simply aging.

I can't run away from aging. But I can massage it out like a ball of dough and then sprinkle on fairy dust and hope for the best. And when I go to sleep, oiled up enough to effortlessly roll down a Slip 'N Slide, I think, *This is what "going with the flow" must mean for people who do things like that.*

Marrying a Criminal on the Run

It's my express dream to meet someone in witness protection. I will nod knowingly at them one day, when their story becomes too winding and they accidentally leak an important detail. I'll smile widely and wink at them. And then they'll know that I know that they're in witness protection. And no words are ever exchanged. The innocents can still be protected.

I worry that if I were to speak this wish out loud, to someone in witness protection, they could be in danger. Or, I could be in danger. Or, we could be in danger, together. Which might be worrisome, but also provide rich fodder for the sequel to this book.

I worry that if they were in witness protection, and they thought the wink meant something other than "I know you're in witness protection and we do not need to discuss this further," the wink might be insidious and create unplanned consequences. Rapidly, they might fall in love with me. Then, I could accidentally get married and become a mere cover wife.

Because of this deep-seated worry about becoming a cover wife for someone in witness protection, I have instituted a new policy: criminal background checks for anyone I am seriously dating.

Now, I'll let you in on a little secret. I did this once. I thought it might scare someone away, but I ended up accidentally married to them, anyway. The scare tactic wasn't as effective as it should have been. Subsequently, some years hence, the marriage dissolved.

I worried about writing that line for four years. So, I hung this manuscript out to dry and just lived, which was worrisome in many ways, least of which was: how might I finish this manuscript if I can't even finish a relationship up until death do us part?

The thing is, death is really an extreme way to end a relationship. Divorce is a cheaper, safer alternative, if you think about it. I mean, for them and for me. It's kinda like a giant win-win no one is talking about when they're worried about assets and divisions and alimony. All good things to worry about, to be sure.

Now single, I still worry about being a cover wife, or accidentally getting married again. It's a fear that keeps me up at night. There's really a gap in dramatic comedy to thoroughly explore the topic of "women who lie awake afraid of accidental lifetime legal commitments."

I've been proposed to only eight times now, and the eighth was a joke (I think). "Do you think it's normal to be proposed to this many times?" my friend snidely asked me. "How should I know?" I said. "Well, at least you only married two out of eight, and left the other six out to dry." "I couldn't marry them all at once," I reminded her. Sometimes the law is helpful for things, like insulting against bigamy. Unless you're in Utah.

So, I have instituted a strict protocol to move forward with my life: worry first, date later. I think this will solve a lot of challenges for me. If I just think hard enough and worry the most, I'll be totally unattractive and no one will want to date me, anyway, let alone fake an engagement to me as proposal number nine in the collection. Thus, saved by the worry bell, I won't have to interact with other humans on a so-called "date," over a transactional meal, filled with banal conversation about topics I am either a) not interested in or b) inherently worried about already. There's hardly a happy medium here.

An alternative to the no-dating protocol would be to have prospective suitors date my parents. If they're crazy enough to agree to this crackpot scheme, then they would have to spend time with my parents. After extensive exit surveys, if they all collectively agree this is a worthwhile endeavor, only then would I meet them. I think this would save everyone substantial time and money, except maybe for my parents. But they would most likely do this to avoid having to spend another frigid holiday season with a less-than-warm son-in-law. The one where they nicely, seriously asked me, "Are you really sure about this one? Because we'll support you either way as long as you're sure." I hate eating the words "you were right" so often. It gives me indigestion.

The next protocol is that a background check is still in good order. Five years ago, they cost $17.95 on the Internet with a monthly recurring fee. I worry about the person who subscribes and continues to background check their neighbors, friends, congresspeople, PTA members, pastors, and the like. When I put it that way, to play devil's advocate, I do worry we don't background check enough people. Maybe the recurring membership does deliver some value, upon reconsideration.

Did you realize that you can background check anyone for this small fee? I thought about this when I took my last job, since they did not run a background check on me. It's hard to track me as I've moved seventeen times since the age of seventeen and I keep getting accidentally married and changing my name like the sham feminist that I am. I look like an FBI fugitive on paper, which is really the same thing as being a writer if you think about it. Truthfully, I considered re-upping my membership on this very dodgy website to run a background check on my future boss. I think telling him that I ran a background check on him would have set our relationship up in a scared-straight prison drama quite well. "I know your minor traffic infractions, sir," I would say. "You can't pull one on me."

The final protocol of insurance against being an accidental cover wife is that I have a list of ten people who must vet a future suitor. They would possess full veto power upon reaching a consensus decision. If one person has a legitimate claim against the beau, the bow tie comes untied, and I tell them to hit the road.

Dating me should scare people as much as entice them. Only then would we be on an even playing field, once they understand there are multiple layers of safety protocols, vetting steps, background checks, *Date My Mom* television plot lines, puppeteers of my happiness, outsourced romance police, and things like that to worry about every step of the way. It gives me heart palpitations to realize someone I might love in the future could read this.

At least I'm the absolute, authoritative poster child on "truth in advertising." I'd drink to that. Alone…While eating pasta in bed, and drinking wine out of an adult sippy cup, which is how I spend all Friday nights, if you must know.

Sometimes, I take a brief hiatus from my own worrisome thoughts, which is radically uncomfortable and almost feels like a frontal lobotomy, but I try to do it anyway in the name of experimentation and expansion and what-have-you. So, I made you a very short list of things I do not tend to worry about very much, if at all.

The not-so-very-worried list:

Losing Your Memory

The beautiful escape of a memory erased is that you don't remember what you've lost. You don't remember what you had. Comparisons between then and now, us and them, disappear on the horizon. This seems like a lovely way to be present.

If I can't remember it eventually, perhaps that's also okay. Maybe there is a resignation to forgetting. Maybe it can feel soft and sweet, like going quietly into a starry night sky. Hopefully it includes escaping the pressures of having to track a calendar, birthdays, anniversaries, addresses, aliases, purchases online, remembering to floss, who you've told all of your secrets to, whether or not you procured the copyright to your poems, and the like.

Outliving Your Spouse

The simplest way to do away with this worry is to get divorced. Then you can live alone, drink alone, travel alone, dine alone, hike alone, road trip alone, read alone, eat the whole bowl of French fries alone, drink the whole bottle of champagne alone, bathe alone, get a couple's massage alone (so you have two masseurs at once, a novel idea), walk romantically on the beach alone, speak to yourself alone, write alone, and generally exist alone, alone, alone before the death part of 'till death do us part.

I'm not a fan of aggrandizing divorce per se, but I think the benefits have not been fully, publicly explored. Trust me, people talk about it in private. And by that, I largely mean me, myself and I when we pregame before a family party wherein I show up as the solely divorced black sheep and am usually reduced to tears by the appetizer course.

The second option is to take out a life insurance policy. Easy. It is astonishing that you can take out a policy against someone else's life force energy, and think there's a mathematician that somehow aggregated their life expectancy and eventual demise.

Actuaries are enlightened.

They don't worry.

They have math for that.

Retirement Income

I worry I'm not good at much. Or, as a woman, I worry I won't be wanted past my youth. Which, with Botox and all, is about sixty-five now. Because thirty is the new twenty, forty is the new thirty, fifty is the new forty, sixty is the new fifty I don't even know when you get old anymore. I worry I won't know I'm old until I'm actually old. Is there a way to be told that I'm old ahead of time?

The point is, I have a plan. I'll go pick pineapples in Hawaii. I'm short. The plants are short. I have a low center of gravity, they have a low center of gravity. I think this is my ideal income stream for aging out of the world gracefully and with a full plate of fruit. The weather is just right. I suppose this is the right time to proclaim I do actually like piña coladas and gettin' caught in the rain. And, I have half a brain. For now.

Death

Death is the only thing I can't out-run, out-worry, or out-think.

I empirically, factually, fully know I will die.

So will everyone you know and love.

And so will you.

Some things are better stated in black and white. There you go.

Chapter 2

Let's Worry about Parents

Remember peer pressure in middle school? "Peer" can be a relative term the less you start getting carded at a restaurant when you clearly don't look a day over twenty-two and your friends still get carded when they look several days over twenty-nine. I don't like to be associated with the people who are carded more often than me while they are obviously more affected by the aging process. I say "thank you" every time I am carded. "I'm in that tender transition age," I say as I nod knowingly and hand over my identification card.

Regardless of the illustrious number of half-years away you are from actually turning thirty (the time when the biological clock apparently starts to tick), you might feel continued pressure to worry about what type of parent you'll become the more you realize that your fertility is a time-sensitive, once-in-a-lifetime endowment. Female fertility is not a perpetual annuity. It's more of a reserve; a special type of port you have to down all in one bottle, or else it won't keep to the next day. Both fertility and port are scarce resources. There are no limitless deposits at the bank of feminine potency, and sadly, there aren't limitless options for superbly crafted, barrel-aged digestifs.

Of course, worrying about fertility at thirty-something is mostly a uniquely urban concern, as I understand it. Had I been reared in a more rural context, I would likely have 3.5 kids already, be on a Parent Teacher Association board (I have to do something bossy no matter what iteration of life we're supposing), drive a minivan, own a charming house with rain gutters that are in need of repair, and make a yearly trek to a theme park to eat ethnic food at their international food court. The latter point is because I wouldn't have lived in a densely populated urban center where English was spoken in third place, behind Korean and Spanish. And wherein I could eat my way around the world from the comfort of my own couch, being exposed to 24-hour takeout from far-flung places like South Korea (not to be confused with the North), El Salvador, Greece, Turkey, Lebanon, Northern Italy (not to be confused with the South), Singapore, and Ethiopia. Perhaps the secret to raising the birthrate of babies in urban centers is to remove convenience food. Then people would copulate more instead of just eating themselves into a stupor. Something for our legislators to consider with declining birth rates and shrinking cities.

Like any future, hopefully not-so-bad parent, I already worry that I won't be a decent parent. Which, I dearly hope will make me at least an adequate attempt for a parent, if simply on the merit of pre-worrying that I might be a P.O.S. (AKA, a piece of $*%&).

What I really worry about is how I'll be typecast as a parent, bound to play a role with a certain voice and purpose, shackled to my own expectations of my best-parent self without being able to fully deliver.

Here are the parent traps I foresee, and they're on my list to worry about:

The Facebook Parent | The I-Keep-Tabs-On-Everyone Parent

Joining the largest social engine on the planet, you're a steady adopter of all the right trends, timelines, and tones. You read the right articles. You have coiffed the right style. Your awareness is stunningly on display for all to see how engaged, enlightened, and expanded you are. The inherent calendar features mean you never forget a birthday, anniversary, or important memory from seven years ago. Things are tidy and about connection for you.

You have a life cadence that makes sense.

You keep tabs on everyone and everything but continually have the wrong arguments with the wrong people. You refuse to see your own voice in an echo chamber 'cause your thumbs are scrolling too fast to register the social sonar.

The Instagram Parent | The Picture-Perfect Parent

Life is poised. Positioned. Perfect. You capture the greatness in the moment, even if it is slightly staged. You are adept at angles and positioning, so much so that a selfie might look like a passerby casually snapped you looking luxurious with your baby looking directly into the camera. Operant conditioning works well for both babies and pets to teach them the proper fish lip or eye-popping gaze required for such a moment.

You curate opportunities to share your picture-perfect life with others, so long as they do not poke behind the façade of your fabulously styled, markedly matching family gallery.

The Twitter Parent | The I-Am-Hip-To-Pop-Culture Parent

You live in sound bites and pithy, epigrammatic maxims. You can't stand to have a meandering conversation on life and philosophy unless it is broken down into a few digestible syllables and coined with a marketing hashtag. You live experiences with these hashtags, shuffling your children and your significant other into just the right kind of lighting for the snapshot-worthy moment.

You are quick to fly to the next activity for your children that will bolster their self-esteem or help them win friends and influence people, even if they are still only six.

The LinkedIn Parent | The Achievement-Focused Parent

We focus on achievement above pleasure in America as obsessively as other cultures focus on wrapping just the right ingredients into a piece of bread or dough. Tacos, empanadas, gyros, pierogies, dumplings... Some of the most wondrous food experiences come wrapped. But you, sir or madam Achievement Parent, could care less for the pleasure of a sumptuous, warm, dough-filled anything. You care about progress, achievements, checkmarks, benchmarks, grades, and letters to convey a sense of purpose and identity not just for you, but for your offspring. So, help them.

Your children will be the preeminent students in each class. They will be the champions of whatever they set their minds to, and they will gain entrance into the most prestigious schools and occupations. They will be leaders, change agents, world shapers. I just wonder if they manage to be children for a brief moment during all of this collegiate prep work which starts at preschool.

The Pinterest Parent | The I-Dominate-Domesticity Parent

Your home is a production studio with all members of your family as the supporting cast. The bunts are bunted and the cupcakes are cupped, everything looking domestically divine. The desire is less about enjoying the moment and more about proving you can and will—handily, effortlessly, selflessly—out-do everything with your over-done parties. Forget triangle sandwiches from Costco and premade artichoke dip. You, crusader of the cooking kingdom, will grow your own artichokes. (Note: they take almost a year, which was mildly depressing to me to learn recently but explains the high price tag. Side note to my note: I love that aioli is simply a fancy name for mayonnaise sauce, which is my artichoke dipping vehicle of choice.)

You arrange a magazine-worthy life and home. But are you present enough to enjoy the gift of now? That's why they call it the present, after all—because it's a gift—or so my dad has reminded me many times in bouts and spurts of worry.

There are probably many other lovely tropes available for other parenting styles. It seems there's a style for everyone—you can shop for whatever suits your fancy on the Internet, a dangerous place for pregnant people, probably. (I've never been pregnant, just a lifelong hypochondriac. I don't even need to tell you that out loud because Google already knows it.) Preferring to focus on the things I don't resonate with, attachment parenting freaks me out the most. I'm not sure I could commit to being physically attached to a micro-human for a year after carrying them inside me for quite a few months. French parenting emphasizes gastronomic awareness circa age nine months. This, friends, I could get behind. I worry French infants know more about seasonal vegetables than I do.

Being that I am single, unmarried, unattached, not dating, and sitting at home writing a book about worry instead of participating in the world to get more items to worry about, I realize I am still a far cry away from a baby's cry.

There's more to worry about as you age than simply your parenting style. What if you never have kids? What if you never want to have kids? What if you decide one day to evolve your relationship with your own parents? What if they decide to move in with you or you move in with them?

I did decide to move in with my parents, as an adult. Twice. Both times, after a divorce. If you're not a math person (I'm not) and you're still able to count to two, you'll realize I've been divorced twice, by the age of thirty. It's expensive and not recommended.

I worried that when I moved in with my parents, I would feel I took a giant step backward. The first time, in my twenties, I did. I was devastated, heartbroken, so tired I could barely worry or write down my worries (which, for me, is a real sign of decline). I thought I had made all the wrong life choices; chief example, I bought a lovely little cottage in my early twenties and had to sell it as part of the asset liquidation. When I retell this story in real life, I assert I bought a house in my early twenties and soon after flipped it for a six-figure profit. Which is also true. Stories are interesting like that; many points of view, depending on how much pessimism or optimism the author is choosing to feel that day. After the house sold to the third bidder, after falling out of escrow twice and nearly giving me a stomach full of ulcers, I moved in with my parents. Then, I proceeded to move out from my parents' as fast as possible, with my head still spinning, making long-term decisions and commitments that ended up being extremely costly.

The only person who wins economically in a divorce is the therapist and the lawyer. I should have thought about this more when creating a career that was perpetually based on desperate need... Divorce lawyers. Divorce therapists. One firm: legal and legacy. "Ditch your spouse and ditch your depression" could be the marketing slogan.

Moving in with my parents the second time, in my thirties, was a much different story. I embraced it. I let them cook for me. I sat by the fire and listened to vinyl records from the 1970s with them. We went on long walks. I baked for them, because it's nicer baking for multiple humans than baking for yourself as a solo human. (Plus, I worry if I baked for myself alone, I'd never stop eating.) It was so nice having three hot meals and not be in prison, I thought I might stay indefinitely. "How long are you staying?" my parents would ask. "For eternity, y'all. Buckle up!"

When anyone asked me during my parental homestay what I was going to do with my life, I replied with a cheeky smile, "Nothing." I actually like lowering everyone's expectations of me so there's no way to disappoint anyone, even me, if I do *something*. Anything. It's better than nothing. I'm finally learning about the possibilities of under-promising and over-delivering.

Maybe it still feels like you need to change to fit in with your parents. Or, rather, you need to modify yourself to meet their monstrously large expectations of you. Maybe one parent was tepid lukewarm, and one was stickier than a stalactite on a cave wall. Maybe your mom was a tiger, or your dad was a bear. Maybe this is the plot of *Jungle Book*.

I worry that one day I'll have my own house and my own style and my own voice and my own art. And maybe no one will like it, nor will they like me. So I've built a fictional case study about how those worries will play out with my own fake family who doesn't exist and my own real parents who do exist:

You might find yourself at thirty-five, married with two children, living in a home that you purchased. Your parents fly in for a visit. You ask them to stay in the guest room, which simply means an air mattress on the floor of your son's bedroom. You combine your kids into two rooms, jam the parents into the third bedroom, and try to drown the entire visit with stolen sips of spiced liquor that you've hidden in your bathroom cabinet.

Your chief worry before they arrive is scrubbing your house of its personality. You take down any paintings or pictures that might evoke a visceral response from your parents that the subject matter is offensive, sexual, or otherwise indicative of any viewpoint that they themselves might not hold. Instead of holding fast and true to the person you've become, the uniquely separate and wholly mature adult with your own tastes, desires, and preferences, it's easier for you to scrub your own personality.

Wiping the walls of their usual adornment is like scrubbing a part of your soul with bleach. It's safer and less confrontational to avoid a discussion on art, philosophy, politics, and life with relatives than to maintain your sense of personhood by decorating your own mortgaged house the way you please.

The cycle of shame is worrisome. You find shame in who you have become. It is shameful to present your house and yourself to the world, so you sanitize your sanctuary.

Your own children watch this mad scramble to hide your home's personality and character and internalize this shame themselves. They hear you snickering about your parents' values and not "understanding" you, and subconsciously you worry that they think they will one day have to hide from you.

By refusing to confront our own shame, we perpetuate the cycle.

I worry that we find out too late that it was up to us the whole time to either live or die under our parents' expectations. That we waited too long with untapped power sitting inert, outside of our bodies and our reach, to realize our own power and potential. We were worried that we would be consumed by others' expectations, but it was truly the worry itself that became the all-consuming flame.

I worried that this chapter would be exclusively focused on parental expectations and the burden of hope they place on our backs from the cradle to the grave. But, I forgot for just a minute that I'm in the actual driver's seat now. Actually, that last sentence cost me approximately $5,000 and five years of psychotherapy to blurt out.

The truth is, I occasionally step out of myself, and I worry about my parents themselves, at times. They must have worried about you at one time or another, so it only seems fair to worry about them back. That's reciprocity right there.

What worries me most about my parents is their frailty.

Parents are pillars. They are protectors. They are providers. And, one day, to my greatest dismay and eternal worry, no longer with us. I don't mean that they die, although most tend to do that. I mean that they aren't always there to shield us, protect us, to coach and guide us.

Some parents didn't actually want to take on the badge and title of parenthood and duck out early. Some parents are honestly horrible. Some are abusive and mean. Some are apathetic and unavailable. Like any species, there is a spectrum of parents ranging from the best you'll ever get, to decently tolerable, to horrible and wretched—all of which resemble your 2:00 a.m. takeout options.

I worry that parents feel unneeded and unwanted when the time comes for kids to leave the nest. That their sage wisdom is less spicy the more miles away we move. Of course, they want you to fly away, financially, if nothing else. I worry that some people in my generation are deceived on this economic point.

I worry that I will forget the key lessons that my parents felt necessary to impart. I worry that I will not remember their voices when they are gone, and that I won't feel their guiding presence when I am parenting and aging myself.

I worry that I will bury them, and I am sure one of their biggest and ugliest worries is that they will somehow outlive me and bury me. We worry, mutually. Maybe that's part of what makes a family.

I worry that I will forget how to make chicken chalupas or potato leek soup or persimmon cookies the exact way my mom does. I worry I'll never be able to keep the house as clean or the cars as orderly and functional or lawns as manicured as my dad does. My mom is better at numbers than me, my dad is better at fixing things than I am. I worry I'll miss having them teach me more things.

I worry I'll forget their stories, so I thought about just following them around everywhere with my cell phone and recording their voices at random. But they would likely protest this if they knew, so I won't tell them, obviously. Instead of being a creepy recording artist, I'll save all of their voicemails to me. This way, I will always have snippets of their voice saying, "Hi, I was just thinking about you." Isn't that all we really want—someone to think about us and say it out loud? That's love. Don't tell 'em this, but I rarely pick up when they call because I want them to leave me one more message that just says, "I love you."

Worries aside momentarily, I know I'm the luckiest gal on this side of the Mississippi. Frankly, because I have no idea what happens on the other side of the Mississippi. Knowing that there are at least two human beings in this world fighting for me to survive and possibly thrive makes my heart swell with pride and eyes filled with moisture when I think of all the worrying I have yet to do for my parents. I consider myself the most fortunate person in the world to have felt this energy and love through and through.

I worry that my parents will get Alzheimer's and forget me. I worry they will get even just a mild case of dementia and forget my name. I worry that they will get cancer or another disease that will slowly wreak havoc on them from the inside. I worry they will eat too much red meat and have high cholesterol and rising blood pressure. I worry I won't enjoy the times they cook the filet mignon because I'm worried about their heart or kidneys or whatever I'm supposed to worry about when people get old.

You think your parents spend all this time worrying about you, but honestly, sometimes I fear I spend more of my time worrying about them.

I worry they won't let me into the hospital room when it's time to say goodbye, and it will be too late. I worry they will be mad, but presumably they won't stay mad, when I show up anyway.

We know so much more about aging and health, and yet the worry piles up the more you know. You don't just go quietly into the dark, anymore.

Maybe it is our hubris that pushes us for continual knowledge, even when it makes us feel uncomfortable to realize that our own mortality is illuminated in greater depth when we push the boundaries of what we do know.

And, what we know is our frailty; the fragility and fleeting nature of our own time clock, and the time that others we love spend on this Earth. The frailty of a moment... Of a parent who becomes your friend. Or the frailty of time and space, and our inherent lack of control over the elements that decide our time clock's expiration.

We dream, we hope, as parents. We dream, we hope as adult children that our parents know the depth of love that they have for us is multiplied into the universe, and brought back tenfold through the ticking, tender, tenuous frailty of time we have to spend together.

Chapter 3

Let's Worry about Education

There is so much to worry about when you invest over twelve years in a system that is supposed to transform you into a more well-rounded human being. I went the distance myself and spent twenty straight years in school. It's almost like a prison sentence—"I did my twenty years," I say—except that prisoners are guaranteed three meals a day. College students are another story.

One of the chief aspects of concern with this time investment is whether or not what you learned in school is true. Take the five-paragraph essay, for example. This is the hallmark of your high school writing career. You perfect the introduction, three complementary points, and a punchy conclusion. These essays are copied into your English, History, Economics, and Government classes, and used as the foundation for college applications. The writing formula becomes so routine, it's second nature.

Then, on the first day of English 101 at the collegiate level, you're told, "If I ever see you turn in a five-paragraph essay, you're toast." Honestly, I've never been deliciously crisped with heat on all sides and slathered in butter, so I'm not sure what that insult does for me, specifically. But I suppose in the context of English 101 adjunct professors, who you'll come to find out still eat Top Ramen since their education career took them infinitesimally longer with less earning potential than, let's say, a restaurant manager, you take their insult to heart and shatter your perception of writing forever.

And it seems that toast is only the beginning. Education is one heartbreak like this after another.

You never know, for certain, if what you are learning is true. You'll be torn between your teacher's bias and favor. What if you like one teacher, but detest their opinion? How much subjectivity is allowed in the learning process? How much should the professors hide their bias to allow you to discover the "truth," and really, who defines this truth in total when all is said and done?

The most objective aspect of education is how much it costs one to procure an education. I'm not talking about higher education, here. The thing is, we don't all come out of public, private, or alternative K-12 schooling with the same notions and ambitions.

So, let's worry about each scenario individually.

Public School

I didn't attend public school myself, but a majority of my peers, friends, colleagues, and loved ones all did. Basically, everyone I know, but me. So I'll do my very best to put myself out there and worry about things I have never personally experienced myself, nor ever will as a student. This type of unbiased, inexperienced gesticulation about subjects I am not an expert on is honestly the trademark of quality worrying. It's like next-level worrying right there.

Some of my concerns with public school are obvious, and maybe you've worried about these already. Things like bullying, drugs, not fitting in, peer pressure, etc. But I think your chief concern should be the money in your parents' pockets, as well as worrying about the money in everyone else's parents' pockets.

See, the entire operation is supposed to be cooperative and based upon taxation of the community to provide beneficial, equitable services for the next generation. The thing about it is, some parents are better at raising funds than others. Some parents just have a bit more in their pockets to be taxed on and thus schooled with than other parents. The chief worry is *how* is that money flowing to education?

I don't have offspring yet, which is both a worry and an ease of worry. But I do worry what kind of neighborhood I need to afford to buy a house in, which then, in turn, tells me which kind of schools my supposed offspring can supposedly attend. I worry about getting the downpayment to buy the house. I worry about the career track I need to pursue in order to gain such funds in order to worry about the house. I worry about not having enough time to attend the Parent Teacher Association meetings or volunteer for school picture day (pre-dreading, already), since I am consumed with the career track that pushed me to buy a house in the better neighborhood with the better schooling options. I am worried that after the schooling is over, and the offspring are launched out of the nest, that I will wonder where the time went while I was putting in the hours to gain the career as the years breezed by.

I worry about the other parents I will meet and the teachers that will be a part of this system, hoping there will be mentors, friends, and challengers who will push my offspring to be their very best when I can't coach on the sidelines every day. I hope they will worry about my children when I can't be there to worry in person. I hope I can sub in other good-natured worriers. Isn't worrying a community effort, after all?

I worry that after all that worry, I might have missed something important, special, and fleeting.

Private School

Shortcutting the worry process here by a few seconds, please take all of the economic, budget, and career-mapping worries from the public school diatribe and lay them out here, as well. The same money woes still apply here.

My worry about private school is slightly more nuanced. I worry about homogenization. I worry about a lack of cultural diversity leading to a lack of sensitivity to other belief systems and ways of seeing the world. I worry that sameness leads to blindness.

I worry that the bubble of private school sends the message to the recipients of that education system that there is limited scope to consequences. That any unpleasant "situations" can be contained if your parent(s) donate enough money. That your consequences are not reverberated and felt beyond the scope of someone's benevolent, but woefully misguided, bailout.

I'm not simply talking about high school. I'm talking about bailout programs and subsidies for college-aged (read: legal adults) decision-making. I have personally spoken with or seen students of private colleges committing illegal acts, and the school choosing not to report such acts to the authorities. I worry that maybe more than a few people understand that the easiest place to run a drug scheme is in a private college—be remorseful, honest, sincere, and grovel when you get caught. Get a mentor. Write an essay. Apologize profusely. Don't absorb the legal consequences because you have been taught to shield yourself from outside judicious authority for quite some time. Play the game, and play it well, and avoid consequences at any cost for as long as humanly possible.

I worry that more than a few people understand this scheme of consequence abatement and avoidance when it comes to date rape and drugs. And I worry that makes all of our campuses, and the lives of our daughters and our sons, a little less safe every day in this exclusive bubble that costs an arm, and a leg, and a kidney, and maybe your grandmother's social security number, for good measure.

Alternative School (AKA, Homeschooling and Unschooling)

There's more to worry here than what meets the eye. There is a lack of oversight that is particularly alarming for folks who tend to like words like "*regulation.*" I can't say whether or not I'm a fan of regulation, but the 3 Rs—reading, 'riting, and 'rithmetic—seem like hallmark cornerstones of an educational system here in the good 'ole U.S.A.

The thing to worry about with alternative school is that you might find yourself being homeschooled by the most well-meaning but scattered parent who forgot to teach you to be actually literate. You go through a seemingly normal childhood, raising goats, ducks, and chickens on an urban farm, and living in seeming harmony with your unregulated environment. You play outside occasionally, when you turn off the TV, and are only mildly vitamin D deficient. You are pre-diabetic because you forgot to eat nutritious food and don't know what vitamins and minerals are, but that honestly could have happened to almost anyone in America. Don't feel too bad about that last point.

Everything appears to be gravy. You roll through high school with minimal disruption to your scheduled activities of living at home, having close relationships with your under-employed parents, and watching TV with your siblings most of the day because you don't have a built-in social routine. Trouble is, once you enroll in the local community college after graduating with a legally recognized diploma, you can't seem to pass any of the remedial classes for English or Math. With the lowest bar being eighth grade competency, you soon realize that you didn't learn too much after the age of twelve, or in seventh grade.

You worry that you're functionally illiterate, because you are. And this isn't exactly your fault. You are now technically old enough to go to the library every day and enroll in private tutoring, but you can't seem to get the motivation to get out there since you've spent the last six years in an intellectual malaise. It could be called "unschooling," what you endured, no one bothering to tell you that there are certain critical life skills you need to build in order to be gainfully employed in this current economy. Namely, speaking and basic math. And, between the two options, I'd worry not enough people value the speaking part.

I worry that the readers might think I am condemning homeschooling and combining it with unschooling. I'm not. The two are different. Homeschooling can provide structure, rigor, and academic achievements far surpassing the caliber of public school. However, the standards are set by individual parents who may or may not have the time or capacity to teach. Unschooling is the belief that the child will inevitably discover what they need to know for themselves, somehow, if the right environment were produced.

Honestly, I wish that I would discover what I need to know about cooking the perfect steak dinner if only the right environment were created, but sometimes it's such a nice treat to have the

Barefoot Contessa just tell me how to do it. Then I don't have to worry about how all the ways that eating undercooked red meat can kill me. Or, even easier yet, I'd rather just have a sumptuous steak feast delivered to my doorstep.

I worry we're getting off track now that I'm thinking of ordering in food. You can't really say ordering takeout, since you're ordering the takeout to be taken to you. I can casually say, but I can't type that I'm thinking of ordering food in, since hanging prepositions are a real big no-no (that's the official term). Is it dinner time yet?

Public school, private school, and alternative schooling are key debates for K-12. Then there's the worry of continuing education. Should you pursue training via trade school? A bachelor's degree? What about becoming a doctor, lawyer, or business executive (some of which require advanced degrees)?

I opted for the latter route because I'm a glutton for punishment and did not have a solid plan in life. What really rang my bell is that my younger, smarter, less-in-debt brother opted for the former route. He went to trade school and was making substantially more income than me per year than several years after I finished my Master's in Business Administration. MBA, of course, meaning Much Bull&*% Absolutely. It's a lesser-known business degree wherein you acquire the necessary skills to be a politicking middle manager in corporate America and maximize your 401(k) contributions to reduce tax liability, while draining your life energy one blood droplet at a time in the name of consumerism.

One of my favorite get-to-know-you questions is, "What do you wish you would've studied in university?" Of course, this is audience specific to people who like to wax poetically about the past and who likely have acquired useless degrees like myself and done something totally different than what they studied. (I'm not alone here, people.) I oft answer that I would've studied anthropology, astronomy, or archeology. I like alliteration.

Obviously.

The cracker jack truth of the matter is that I studied what I studied when I studied it because I liked it (eww, not the MBA, that was out of a directionless grasping for steadier career prospects). I double-majored in Theology and English Literature in undergrad, with a minor in Humanities. I changed my major an unlucky thirteen times, at least. Might have been more, but I lost the paperwork. I wanted to study everything. I wanted to learn everything. I wanted to be everything. And ultimately, studying the words humans use to discuss the divine (Theology class) and English Literature (sadly, it did not include Russian, African, European, South American Literature or even many Irish or Scottish folks) was a pretty perfect portal into the "everything" I was seeking: words. On my life bucket list is to stop worrying that I studied the wrong thing. Alas, I can't cross everything off the bucket list too early, or else what would I have to live for next?

The bureaucracy of a university system, frankly, is so far beyond me. It operates like a government. Slow, arduous, winding. Committees that form sub-committees to commit to things or un-commit to other things. Paperwork upon paperwork to produce more paperwork while proclaiming it's time to go paperless. At my private university, there were even bird-dogs, watch dogs, and surveillance protocols about which books were allowed to be read on a college campus.

This isn't a joke. I went to university between 2006-2010 and there were banned book lists. In fact, there were so many parent complaints about questionable material, the college professors had to submit their reading list to the Dean of the English Department for approval prior to each semester. Of course, in the name of fighting fascism, I found a subversive approach to free book acquisition: *interlibrary loan*. A genius program wherein I could live at a university with a banned book list, and magically order books from Berkeley, Stanford, and other libraries to read stuff I wasn't supposed to learn at my own school. Remember, I was a college student. A legal, voting-age, can-buy-tobacco adult.

I read and read and read. Sometimes I worried I would miss class because I was hiding out and reading banned books. My favorite reading spaces were clandestine enterprises where no one could find me and no one could ask what I was doing. For the outdoor variety, I would linger under a pine tree in the middle of my suburban Los Angeles campus, which enveloped me like a canopy while I crouched in the dirt to learn stuff. Or, I would skulk down three flights of abysmally unkempt stairs and wedge myself in between the stack of rolling bookshelves in the basement of the library where no one went. Smelling vaguely of mold, the thing to worry about was whether someone might roll me to death between bookshelves. It was sneaky and fun and even dangerous, and no one knew about it. Except, perhaps, the astute librarian.

The trouble was, I had so many banned things to learn and topics to cover outside of class—while keeping my GPA up and running around to my four different part-time jobs—that I would forget to return the books. I had an entire out-of-class curriculum that was rigorous and fresh and invigorating. It made it a bit confusing why I was paying to go to class, albeit I did learn some things there, too. I wish I could tell you all the things I learned by myself and the ways I got in trouble for saying some of them, but there's even a moratorium on that, I suppose. I racked up over $150 of library fines. Which meant, until I paid them, I could not graduate.

Now, at the time, $150 was a lot of money. So the best day of my college life was when I got an email that said "library fee jubilee." This is the practice of debt forgiveness from the Bible. A donor provided a fund to forgive literate laggards their fines. One catch: I had to write an apology letter and present it to the librarian in person.

The ethics of this stunned me. I was honored to receive a get-out-of-jail free card, collect $200, and pass graduation "go." I was graduating into the 2008/2009 recession, so there was literally nothing for me to look forward to, except legally imbibing gin, but my bubble hadn't burst yet. And I didn't know what a gin gimlet was yet, either. But I was sure relieved to get this news of jubilee, as I didn't think my parents would take kindly to the news that they could not attend my graduation as the first college graduate in my family due to my habitual pattern of loving books more than people and holding on to them for far too long (I mean, holding on to the books, not to the people).

But I wasn't really sorry. I didn't know how to make a sincere apology. I wanted to tell them that this was my political resistance against their lackluster literacy practices which deemed books "bad." I wanted to decry that being afraid of ideas is the most insidious idea of all; that intellectual censorship is a form of mental castration. I wanted to say, "It's impossible for this book to be 'bad' since, as a collection of static words, said book does not have its own ontological moral code and anthropomorphic being-ness. They don't. They're just books. Just ideas." And, this was like my own *Fahrenheit 451* moment. I saved the ideas out of the books that were banned. I ate the stories. And the stories became me, and I became the stories. And here I am now. Look at how well-adjusted I turned out.

I waited until the very, very last day of jubilee, almost down to the hour. And I presented the world's shortest apology. "I'm very sorry," I said to the librarian, "for being forgetful." That's it. That's all I could come up with. She was unamused. But she stared at me, through her reading glasses chained to her face. I wanted to say, "I used this time wisely to learn all the things I'm not supposed to know and can't tell you about, anyway." But, I shrugged. I *looked* apologetic (I can do that, at least). And I said, "I'm very, very grateful." Which was authentically, unequivocally, 100% true.

Whilst at one of my many office jobs, someone once told me I was an "educated person" (really took them for a loop, didn't I?), then proceeded to ask me a grammatical question. I responded with a pretentious, but genuine monologue on how the English language and usage of language in general is an evolving, changing, organic, alive, open system. I said the ecosystem of learning and language is a wide open, ever-expanding universe of options. And, so, at times, I continued between dramatic pauses, it felt like it wasn't worth my time to learn to spell a certain word or discern the difference between "affect" or "effect" in a casual work email when there is a whole wide, gigantic, chaotic universe out there begging to be discovered. (At least this pronouncement about language processing wasn't between me and my boss, or I might have worried my waxing poetic about language evolution would have diminished my employment viability.) It was also the last time someone asked me a grammatical question at work. Thank goodness for them and me.

As an aside, I honestly think "grammar" should be spelled "grammer," and I mistype it every single time. I'm one of the world's worst spellers. Watching movies about spelling bees is like acupuncture for me. But, I do it anyway because I like to worry about how bad of a speller I truly am. Honestly, ask anyone, including my junior and high school writing teacher who caught a typo on my first draft of this Table of Contents, no less. Oops. I'm sorry, Mrs. S. Please don't take my spelling failure personally.

The thing is, I've been through more than one of the educational systems listed above and learned to tell the tale. Some would even say I emerged in one piece. That's generous. Or, at least more likely, I learned to worry more than I used to, which is sort of the point of this non-autobiographical conglomeration of thoughts.

The real concern is: did my education teach me to learn? Yes, in my humble case, it did. It taught me to care about the ever-expanding universe and learn how I specifically learn. Learning to learn is the meta takeaway here.

Learning to learn and then maybe, someday, hopefully *loving to learn* seems like the very best achievement of any educational quest.

No matter the economics of your parents, your sheltered decision making, or your current literacy level, learning to love learning is something anyone can access. All you need is a bit of hope, a spark of magic, and a public library card. Or a twenty-year prison sentence. (Read: please don't defund public libraries.)

Chapter 4

Let's Worry about Finding a Career

When I was a senior in high school, my response to the question of what I wanted to do when I grew up was simple: "Get paid to argue." Of course, my parents' friends scoffed at that smart aleck response and told me to prepare for a law school admission test. Obviously, I decided to major in Humanities, ambled my way through a Master of Business Administration degree, and eventually made it so far as to get paid to negotiate contracts. (This was before my illustrious career as a wannabe author, naturally.)

I argue daily. Sometimes I get paid to argue in the form of contract negotiation. Writing is arguing with yourself and eventually translating that argument into copy. I worry, sometimes, that I will run out of things to argue about, or people to argue with. So, that's the main reason I keep my cable and multiple content streaming services accounts alive. The more content I consume, the more shows I have to argue about with people I meet at random. This is my safety net in case the people I already know stop answering my text messages.

My favorite movie the year I graduated with my bachelor's degree was *The Graduate*. I had never resonated with a character so poignantly as I did with Dustin Hoffman's. Not the sexual awakening part, nor the freedom of the open road adventure, just so we're clear. The scene I'm talking about is Dusty at a cocktail party. Having your parents' friends evaluate your life choices over a stiff martini made a lot of sense to me, had I been the type of person who happened to have country club member parents and country club parents' friends. However, blue collar families also have the dreams and aspirations of their children rising above the fray and becoming special, unique, not-so-ordinary creatures, too.

Plastics. They tell Dustin Hoffman's newly graduated character that it's all about plastics. Maybe career advice changed very little from 1967 to 2017. It's about security, plasticity, and liquidity. Honestly, there is *some* life wisdom to the idea of a career that is based on a commodity that 99% of us consume daily here in these fine United States of America. Did you know that manufacturing plastics packaging is the third largest industry in the U.S.A.? I learned that fact at a cocktail party (where else?) from someone whose family makes the official crime scene packages for the government to dispose of dead bodies. Imagine being the authority on death bags. That's a real humdinger of a legacy.

The worry surrounding what you're doing to "be" or "do" with your life starts much earlier than graduating with your bachelor's degree. The worry sets in around fifteen or sixteen, for most. Depending on your household income and what zip code you live in, your worry will be different. Will you go to college? Will you get an apartment? Will you get married and start a family?

You're supposed to have guidance to help you make these decisions and alleviate some of this worry. Allegedly, these people exist. They are called guidance counselors in high school or career counselors in college. Those who can't do, teach. I wonder and worry if the adult career counselors can actually work outside of telling other almost-adult people how to have a career. Think about it. It's a bit of a strange occupation to work in a high school or collegiate career center and spend your entire career telling other people how to go get one. "Well," I would say, "if it were as streamlined and easy as you say it is, wouldn't you have a career yourself?"

Your senior year of high school is fraught with worry. It's hard to think of a time that is laden with more decision-making burden than your senior year, a time where you have limited resources, agency, and wisdom but make some of the most impactful decisions of your entire life (to date). You can't legally smoke or drink alcohol, but you can operate death machines known to pedestrians as cars. You might be old enough to be sent to war by the time you're a senior in high school, but you can't complete a form for federal financial aid without your parents' income information tacked on. You are at once set free to decide the trajectory of your life, without any legal coping mechanisms for stress.

It's like you are a child again, stuck and sinking in the sweaty jungle pit of balls at your neighborhood fast-food restaurant. You have to find the one purple ball in a sea of blue, yellow, red, and green balls. There might be hundreds of balls, and there is only one purple ball with the Magic 8 answer of what you should do with the rest of your life. You might never find the purple ball. You might expend all of your energy searching for the purple ball. Or, you might figure out, eventually, that if you somehow combine the red and blue balls you can create a new purple ball. Synergy. Innovation. Add some more corporate buzzwords here.

See, I worry that when you're under tremendous pressure at seventeen or eighteen to make a decision for the rest of your life, you don't know the most important inputs. You focus on output. What will you do? Who will you become? But the real question is: what skills do you need to gain in order to figure out that answer?

Here are all the things that you should worry about when figuring out a career. I tried to preemptively worry about everything for you. I'm worried I left something really salient or dire off of the list, but here you go:

1. Life will pass you by while you are trying to "figure things out." I really feel like this is an underrated trap that is out there for just about everyone. It's like an equal opportunity trap. I mean, you don't want to make a misstep and launch yourself down the wrong path.

2. You make the wrong decision, and your career gets outsourced. You know, it really bugs me that we never hear about in-sourcing. Is there anything else we're good at in the U.S.A. anymore?

3. By committing to one career, you miss out on the next big tech bubble. Or you miss out on whatever big, hot, shiny, new, tantalizing, exotic career would have made you a multimillionaire. Example: you specialize in networking hardware when cloud computer programming takes off, and you miss the code base boat by just a space or a tab. Apparently, not everyone has this ambition to become a multimillionaire. Some people just want to be average middle class, mortgaged, and living life simply like their parents did. But they haven't heard that the middle class is eroding. Hello, this is me. I'm here to give you a new worry: There is no more middle class. It's already gone. Your children won't join it. If you're middle class now, you won't last in its dying, erasing fantasy, either.

4. You get a great job and get laid off before it really turns into a meaningful, lucrative career. This kills your confidence and impedes your libido. There are 1:00 a.m. commercials made just for you. You eat a lot of extra carbs to console your crying cells, and put yourself at high risk for cardiovascular disease and diabetes. From there, you usually attempt to learn more job skills online for free, but because there is no carrot on the stick that is compelling enough, you start, stop, and peter out continually. In the meantime, you can try to shift gears and start a new path. But...on to #5.

5. You get a graduate degree in order to delay the launch of your career. Your sibling who went to trade school makes more money than you since they chose an occupation that people actually want and need, and they didn't incur student loan debt to achieve a six-figure income. You're also out-earned by the local fast-food chain manager who at least has full-time health insurance benefits, dental insurance, life insurance, AD&D insurance, spousal insurance, dependent insurance, supplemental

income insurance, pet insurance and can also afford to purchase any auxiliary up-sell insurance they want out of their own pockets. Essentially, they are insurance connoisseurs, and you are, simply put, "well educated." I really cringe when people call me well educated. How well? Well enough? Well enough in debt? Well enough to know "affect" vs. "effect"? Oops, not hardly. Please, Lord, do not give me more suffering than I bear. Or bare? It's hard to know most days. Etymology is all so Greek to me.

6. You start a career, but you hate it. You stick with it. You end up in therapy, but at least you can afford to pay one measly human being to be your friend for $150/hour, for forty-five minutes per week. This way you know you can tell the truth to one trusted person—the whole truth and nothing but your subjective truth. You can bring in your poetry, do a dramatic reading, and not worry about copyright infringements. You also are paying for your audience. It's a bit of a rigged game, but nonetheless, one you, too, can play. This one person can hold all of your secrets, and is legally bound to confidentiality. I kind of wish I could bind all my friends to legal confidentiality. Here, here's a contract to be my friend: I'll sue you if you say anything about me to anyone. I think that would really set up the friendship with the right tone from day one.

7. You start a job, but it never turns into a career. You show up when you're supposed to, you don't get fired, you say the right things, you get a 3% cost of living raise that just barely keeps you on pace with the Consumer Price Index and rising inflation. You never really feel like you're owning it. You just keep chugging along, though. I feel like you should get bonus points for this attempt, but sadly, the universe doesn't always see it that way. If I could be your fairy godmother because you tried somewhat hard, I would. I'd probably deliver you socks and underwear because that's what a practical, pragmatic, perfunctory godmother of try-hards would give out as gifts.

8. You don't start a career, you only work part-time during seasonal breaks. And your parents hate you. And you hate yourself for living in their basement. But on the upside, most houses don't have basements. At least you're winning in the basement department if you have a basement at all. It could be turned into a fallout shelter. Fall out from your miserable, meandering life.

9. You choose to have a family instead of a career, but you end up divorced. This can be a long-term issue if you don't play your alimony cards correctly. Ideally, you live in a community property state and get divorced prior to year ten of marriage so you can maximize your alimony distribution. Sole custody is the wrong play, here. You should definitely go for fifty-fifty so you can spend 50% of the year away from your said family while eating lobster on the beaches of Mexico. I should've thought of all of this before I got divorced twice and ended up in debt, whilst not owing or receiving alimony. I've definitely done everything in my life wrong. I know that.

10. You choose to have a family instead of a career, and you end up stretched financially for your entire life because it's nearly impossible to live on one income unless your spouse is a magnificent breadwinner. This can cause significant stress. The only salvation is the dollar store. Not the fake dollar store, the $0.99-only store. The Internet might even tell you what to do when you get there to make it look more luxe. You might even be happy.

11. You take a job you love, which turns into a career you have always fantasized about, but you are chronically underpaid and can't save enough to retire comfortably. Or, perhaps you can never retire at all. You are feverishly pouring into others with a career that pays you enough to live in a minimally furnished apartment, and you tell yourself there is more to life than money. So, you defer your student loans a tiny bit longer to keep going to the job that pays you just above minimum wage. But at least it's a job you just *love*. I worry about what we mean by "love," here. I digress.

12. You don't start a career at all. You work casually at the local electronics store. You stream video games and become an Internet sensation for a few years, which ends up earning you an annual six-figure salary. But you forgot to learn about financial literacy during the monetary upswing and ended up spending all of your money. So you go from a net worth of approximately half a million dollars to working at the same electronics store yet again for approximately $0.50 above minimum wage.

13. You launch a business and move internationally to live out your digital nomad dreams, mere weeks before a global pandemic shuts the world down. For a moment—a brief and fleeting moment—you feel widely successful and massively happy, and it all comes crashing down after just twenty-one days.

14. You become an influencer online. A digital tastemaker. You realize that you are working eighty-plus hours a week for about $14,000 a year. Trading time for money is a game that's hard to win. But, you look mighty fine doing it. And doesn't that count for something?

15. Timing isn't in your favor. The economy tanks when you try to launch your career. If you are a millennial, perhaps you graduated college into the worst recession in near American memory (that is, the one a few years hence and prior to the one we might be entering soon). You might have graduated at the top of your university class with Latin Honors to find yourself working slightly above minimum wage selling cosmetics. You take the job because you believe in small businesses making the difference in the lives of everyday Americans, or at least you saw that in a commercial once during election season. You try to make the most of it by contributing with Excel spreadsheets and what your boss terms "computer knowledge." But you might face a small setback emotionally when you're passed up for the warehouse manager promotion by someone who was picked up and jailed for a drug parole violation. They're holding the job open for her; the position will be hers yet again when she finishes the prison sentence. Of course, this is her third violation, so sentencing may take a while. It's not a plotline for a sensational crime television show, it's your tedious life. It could happen to you. Maybe you can sell the story to TV one day, but in the meantime, your used Ford Pinto is having trouble getting you up the hill to work each day as your graduation tassel hangs ominously from the windshield, reminding you of all the delicious life dreams you once held. And you resume inventory by paper because no one wants your fancy computer skills meddling with an inventory process that already "works." Clock in, clock out. Another day, another broken dream. Rudderless in your routine, you slowly begin to deeply understand why the show *Cops* is filmed in New Mexico. You spend Saturday nights wandering aimlessly around big box stores, not buying anything, just to protest consumerism. This is the chapter wherein you take up gin as a hobby and jump on your couch because there are no adults present to tell you not to. You're the adult now. Congratulations, you Magna Cum Laude graduate and two-time winner of *Who's Who in America: Colleges and Universities* during a recession. In the sage words of an ancient Hebrew king, "*Everything is meaningless*" (Ecclesiastes 1:2). You only need to get to the second verse of the book to hear the whole summary: it's all meaningless. All of it. No, I'm not a nihilist, I'm simply quoting the supposed wisest man of ancient days.

There is truly so much to worry about filed under the category of "getting things wrong." However, what if you happen to get it right, and strike it rich with a wonderful, successful, abundant, satisfying, service-focused, longstanding, respectful career? I have you covered, don't worry. I mean, don't worry *yet*. We have so much worrying to do *still*.

Here is a list of everything to worry about if you *do* end up with a career:

1. Your work is your purpose, your purpose is your work. Congratulations, you. You scored. You are a champion. The career is you and you are the career. Without being a naysayer, I'm going to take just a moment to remind you that your cushy, charmed career still might face layoffs, outsourcing, economic depressions, economic recessions, economic shrinkage, economic booms in industries other than your own, global pandemics, political upheaval, violent transfer of power post-elections, diasporas, the erosion of trademark and copyright laws, lawsuits, famine, pestilence, the return of diseases like polio, measles outbreaks at theme parks, ocean temperatures rising, glaciers melting, vegans preaching that all your life choices are killing the planet, cow flatulence, eroding ozone layers, your favorite shows not being renewed, the price of craft beer rising above ten bucks a glass, bans from sitting on the beach, the inability to acquire a domain name of your own name, Internet Terms of Service owning your life force and genetic DNA codes, your children growing up in a global world with a one-world government, alien invasions (probably originating at the Denver airport), and alumni fundraising dinner invites to return to the scene of the crime when you spent over a hundred-thousand dollars on your degree already. Et cetera. No one ever bothers to write it out. You are welcome.

2. It will suck every living last ounce of energy from you. At least you have the income to pay to escape at the spa. In fact, you spend an inordinate amount of time and money at the spa. The spa is your escape of choice. You could nap at home, but why would you? It's much better to pay an absorbent sum of money to nap at the spa to escape your expensive apartment, which you use to escape from your energy-vampire sucking job. It's a systematic process of pay-to-escape. The only rational way to spend your hard-earned money is to pay to sleep in semi-public spaces in the name of recreational relaxation. If you feel spending money to sleep at the spa is a bad idea (don't tell me this because I'm not sure our friendship could survive this news), then the alternative is that you could pay to go take a nap with music. This variety is called a sound bath. It's a collection of relaxation-inducing sounds, instruments, electronic music, and drums complete with a light show. They hand out blankets, pillows, and steaming cups of non-caffeinated herbal tea. I always go with a friend to be both a bodyguard (I mean, sleeping in public is a bit sketchy, I suppose we can all agree on this) and a snore patrol. On that note, I wouldn't say I snore inordinately loud. And she says my snoring is cute, for the record. But it is technically against the studio's policy to be a "snorer." You can sleep, but you cannot snore. I'm not sure what she gains from this arrangement but mostly she stays awake and slugs me in the shoulder every now and again, which gets the snoring to stop but induces a sleepy grunt. A gentle grunt. The grunt means, "Thank you for patrolling my public sleeping," and, "I should probably pay for your mimosa next time we're at brunch." And I do. And so will you. Because you're gainfully employed, and can afford to buy mimosas whenever you want.

3. You end up with a thriving career, but you get divorced, which will erase a lot of your hard-earned money. (In my case, maybe the marriage dissolved because I spent too much time at work.) Or, perhaps it's the fault of your partner who also has a thriving career. I assume the rest of the scenario goes something like this, perhaps, speaking from experience: the two of you have to choose between two competing lives, locations, vocations, and callings— and at the end of the day, you simply can't decide who does the dishes and who cooks. The obvious answer is takeout, but we established you can't order in what is supposed to be taken out. Which is really hard, then, when you have to decide who has to go to the restaurant and pick up the takeout. Or, you disagree on the appropriate amount of throw pillows. The answer is, "However many I am pleased to buy and use to cushion myself as I sit in your presence," but, alas. Relationships have ended over much less.

4. You decide to make work a priority and the years roll by and you're infertile. Some things, like penicillin and cow's milk, truly have a serious expiration date. I suppose I meant this line quite literally when I wrote it, hearing the tock and the tick of my own biological clock. I'm not sure my body got the memo that forty is the new thirty. Should I tell it now? On second thought, infertility could be biological or creative. You might make your work such a priority you forget to nourish your creative soul. It shrivels like a raisin in the sun; no chance to transmute your "ish" into wine. Time, time, ain't on your side. So, you check yourself into creativity rehabilitation and realize that some people's midlife crises come early. Yours could come as early as thirty-one. You overachiever, you. What is *time*, anyway?

5. You retire and realize that all of your friends were coworkers, not friends. This is a tricky thing to worry about, since it calls up our deepest insecurity of wondering if anyone really loves us or needs us to begin with. Speaking of which, I am beginning to think that the only person who is really on my side is my therapist, who I expressly pay to love me and listen to me read my writing out loud and tell me it's good and stuff. I imagine a packed retirement party with cake and champagne. Then, the next week, crickets. Not the kind of crickets covered in chocolate you eat at a street fair to prove that you're adventuresome. I mean, no one calls. No one texts. No one emails. No one sends carrier pigeons to check on you and communicate top-secret messages. Are our relationships placeholders until we move to the next community, job, etc.? Do these people care about you beyond the value you provide for them on a daily basis (if you're one of those "value-adding" employees)?

6. Your career stalls. Nothing bad really happens, but nothing good really happens, either. You are in a purgatory of apathy. You wished you cared more to improve the situation, but the exertion of energy it would take to make a change feels insurmountable. So you consume books, podcasts, self-help books, growth seminars, affirmation tapes, life coaching, talk therapy, online courses, and

spend a small fortune to learn that you should "do what makes you happy." Should-ing on yourself is really unhelpful at this point, too. What if you have no idea what makes you happy? All the self-help stuff in the world seems to assume you already know what makes you feel organized and alive. All of the growth books I've read assume you have a vision. But if you mention it to anyone, "Hey, I don't think anything makes me happy anymore and I don't have a vision for the future," they think you're clinically depressed and ask if you're suicidal. What if you're not depressed and you're just honest? There's little room to admit you aren't happy and you don't know why and you're mildly okay with existing in a blank state for a while. I'm not sure what we could collectively call it, but maybe you can phrase it something like this: "I'm on hiatus from caring about anything, but this isn't a clinical condition. I'll let you know when my give-a-crap button comes back online." 'Till then, go to the beach. It's a place where it's perfectly acceptable to lie around like a dead fish and do nothing while wearing minimal clothing. Anyone who says the sand is an annoyance isn't seeing the bigger apathetic picture here.

7. You live on autopilot. The career is good, the family is good, the house is good. But, nothing is great. You're fine but you're not fantastic, whenever someone asks. Nothing is sensational, seductive, or salacious about your life. Nothing sparks your imagination anymore. You've spent all your decades checking boxes: career, family, house, education, investments, travel, etc. But there is no soul to your list; it is all kitsch. Who invented the checklist, anyway? Were you downloaded this at birth? Is the point only to achieve more success than your parents, if only by a slim margin? (This argument falls apart slightly when you look at statistics of millennials who live at home.) This lifestyle is rich fodder for a midlife crisis—the type of moment where you decide to hit the full-life-reset button and change your career, change your relationship status, change your living situation, change your friend groups, change your hair, change your body weight, change your wardrobe, all in one month's time...and find yourself living alone in a foreign country realizing that sometimes there is no

such thing as incremental change. Occasionally, the Band-Aid has to be ripped off all at once, collateral damage be damned, so you can finally feel something—anything—again. Maybe that's just me. But, I sincerely doubt it. Because when I told the "plan" to a few people, their only response was "I'm jealous."

I asked my mom once, "What happens when all your dreams die?" She said, "Dream new dreams."

But, what if I'm too tired? Dreams are super costly. They are far away, too—farther than the British Nation, or the French Nation—they live in the Imagine-Nation. It's a far-off land that's incredibly difficult to access after some time away. My passport stamp to Imagine-Nation expired. I don't remember the visa process. Can I come as a guest? Do I need to establish residency? What if I just exist, dreamlessly, for a moment? Is that allowed?

The most uncomfortable secret I've learned about careers and life transitions is that there is no meta-narrative. I don't think there's one thing you're "supposed" to do, other than become yourself. Which is tiresome and trying if you don't really know who you are, and unfortunately no one person other than you can discover this. You can't pay your way out of this problem. You can't think your way out of this program. Apparently, it's a matter of the heart. If that organ is still alive in me, I'll drop it a note.

I fantasize about a cosmic vending machine that would hand out life purpose blueprints. Not sure how you'd price this product out, but imagine walking up to a vending machine. You scan your palm. Cosmically registered, you are handed a manual the size of a phone book. Hey, do you remember phone books? Still with me, here? I used them as booster seats and stools in addition to numeric glossaries. Inside the blueprint would contain architectural-style renderings of your perfect house; a caloric permutator with exactly what foods you should eat to maintain your ideal weight; the name, birthdate, and present location of your soulmate (supposing there is just one); a step-by-step guide to earning the exact income you need to meet all of your needs with abundance; and even a set of religious and philosophical beliefs that match your inner longings and spirit. In short, I wouldn't need to discover or do anything other than follow the rules. I just wish I'd be a person who was born to want to follow the rules. The wish falls apart here before I can even finish the daydream.

Most of what I learned about careers and work-type stuff was from the brilliant Chinese military strategist, Sun Tzu. Whenever I would encounter a situation I didn't know how to handle, like managing an unfriendly coworker or planning a dinner party for my extended family, I would consult ancient military strategy. If you met some of my extended family, you'd understand why this was necessary. I don't even need to meet yours to tell you that a military strategy CAN help you create a better family reunion experience for all parties involved. An experience with no violence, fighting, shouting, or reducing people to tears in the backroom during wine "happy" hour. It can also solve almost all of your career problems. Just put some fairy dust on an ancient military strategy, I always say.

Here are some of my favorite military-motivational (AKA, war) quotes:

1. *"Opportunities multiply as they are seized."* I definitely worry I won't seize the right opportunity. What if in the seizing of an opportunity, I miss the better opportunity? This creates a lot of cloudy thinking for me, and the usual remedy is another cup of tea. And as I get older, another cup of decaf tea. Ulcers, much like opportunities, multiply as the caffeine is seized.

2. *"All warfare is based on deception."* Yikes. It's hard to discern if this is more applicable to military strategy, career planning, or dating. I hope it's not true. I worry it is. Is most of our life spent interviewing for jobs or dates to present the best version of ourselves, only to realize that most of the world runs on the interaction fuel of subtle deception? Soft deception occurs all

the time. For example, leading people to think you're a morning person when you're not, or you're a Republican when you're secretly a Democrat, or that you're a Democrat when you're secretly a Republican, or that you're ready to tackle the next big achievement in your career when you'd rather be watching television, or that you're perpetually running five minutes late (when, in actuality, you're very much going to be fifteen-plus minutes late).

3. *"Know thyself, know thy enemy. A thousand battles, a thousand victories."* We're back to this knowing yourself business, which has me a bit queasy. I suppose I thought you would be an adult at eighteen. When I turned eighteen, I thought you'd become a REAL adult at twenty-one. When I turned twenty-one, I looked ahead to thirty. When I turned thirty... I think I just gave up a bit and surrendered, worried I'd never arrive and might as well take a deep breath and live, anyway. I wasn't mad about turning thirty. I didn't dread it. I just realized I had worried for so long about growing up and arriving somewhere else on the horizon. And maybe there's only growing. Not up. Growing. Just moving forward, if you're really lucky. There's also something true about knowing yourself before you try to know someone else. As a kid I always enjoyed putting empty jars and containers back in the fridge only to hear my mom yell, "WHO DID THIS?" Presumably, she knew. Or, how I would hide my vitamin C tablets between the couch cushions because they tasted sour. When my mom found them, she made me eat them. All of them. I hardly got sick again that year after consuming mostly stale, but still viable, pebbles of hardened vitamin C. Maybe knowing yourself is remembering these stories, being able to laugh, and wonder and worry if you'll have kids, will they turn out exactly like you? At least when I have offspring, I'll know to turn over cushions and look out for suspicious vitamin disappearances.

4. *"Hence to fight and conquer in all your battles is not supreme excellence; supreme excellence consists in breaking the enemy's resistance without fighting."* I do like a good breakdown. Like, a musical breakdown. Like an event breakdown after a wonderful

wrap up. A crying, stay-in-bed all day breakdown. I'm not sure I'm the outlaster type. Breaking the enemy's resistance without fighting feels like the last person standing wins. This might not surprise you, but I don't mind cutting my losses and quitting. I don't know if I'm proud of this or simply resigned to the truth of the statement. Or, perhaps I'm the enemy of progress and resistance has simply worn me down. Sunk costs, the money you've paid to generate zero results and get you to "now" are something I've learned to make peace with. Still, I really cling to the idea that I can win a battle without fighting. This sounds like my kind of fray. Just outlast. If I could be the kind of person to summarize the gumption and grit to care enough to do it, I would.

5. *"Victorious warriors win first and then go to war, while defeated warriors go to war first and then seek to win."* Now this is the ultimate fighting quote. WIN FIRST. Enough said. This is the ancient world's version of a mic drop. What victory could be sweeter than that which you taste before the battle even begins? It's kind of like breakfast for dinner. I once asked my mom, with a gleam in my eye, if we could make pancakes, eggs, and sausage for dinner. I was about thirty-one. Maybe it was last week. "Not on my watch," was her solemn reply. I suppose I thought I was victorious with my idea before entering the battle of, "What's for dinner?" I fought first, then lost. I'm really thankful McDonald's started serving breakfast all day (at least where I'm from), and IHOP is available 24/7 in most metropolitan cities for delivery. It's given me slightly less to worry about when I know I can dispatch a human driver to procure me 2,000 calories of food for consumption in one meal, all in the name of breakfast for dinner, at any hour, any day of the week.

So, how do pithy quotes from an ancient military strategist help with one's career? First of all, if you don't want to answer a coworker's question, you can send them a nebulous quote from Sun Tzu. I used to do this all the time. It's better if you can generate a meme, which for posterity's sake I will remind you is simply a picture with a text quote on top, much like an adult's picture book in a single second. Next, if you want to initiate your coworkers during a presentation, you can place Sun Tzu quotes into the slide deck for motivation. I do come from a generation where I learned to make presentations on PowerPoint, look up phone numbers in the phone book, dial 411 for information please, and read about the USSR in 1982 encyclopedias. (This was the 90s, so it was very confusing to me to learn that by the early-90s the USSR no longer existed and Burma is now Myanmar, or vice versa; I'm still confused on this point.) Really, the thing I have in common with both Bill Gates and Elon Musk is that all three of us grew up reading these encyclopedias. For fun. The major difference between us is that I'm not a man. Nor a billionaire. But I will tell you, my first adventure with my driver's license was to the public library so I could check out books published after 1982. Thrilling.

Back to this whole business about careers and what-have-you. So, here's the thing feminism stole from me: the ability to choose to be a housewife. It's unfortunate, because I didn't realize that was a possible, legitimate career option at the time in which I launched myself into the world. I worked. Then I worked some more, got good at asking a lot of questions that seemed to open doors for me, and got my Master of Business Administration degree. And I did work-y things a lot. I joined book clubs with other lawyers, doctors, and business executives, making my life sound like the beginning theme song from the HBO show *Weeds*.

And the rub is, I didn't realize I could have chosen a different path. A path of purpose, peace, pleasure...wherein I didn't have to buy my own bottle service while out and about. Wherein I didn't have to leave the house. Wherein I didn't have to prove my worth through my own personal net worth. Wherein I didn't have to send passive-aggressive Sun Tzu memes to teach other coworkers how to create or avoid drama. The avoidance quote is, ***"Never interrupt your enemy when they're making a mistake."*** I hate even admitting it, but this strategy has served me really, really well.

With the rise of feminism and the idea that women could take over the world, I shouldered this world-domination business quite personally. It was like my own edition of *Atlas Shrugged*, where I thought I single-handedly needed to achieve all the things to prove that a woman could. I'm the first person in my immediate family to graduate with a college degree and then a graduate degree and all that stuffy stuff. Which was cool, and all. Although no one really cares anymore that I majored in whatever-the-heck Humanities program. Whenever someone asks, "What did you study in college?" I look at them lamely, and shrug, "What the heck does it even matter?" I'm not a nihilist, I see this as a pragmatically hopeful response.

In the advent of feminism and feeling like I needed to do it all to prove I could be it all, I realized the one thing I really love is staying home. In exercise clothes. And working out a few times a day. Or going shopping for food. Making food. Thinking about what to eat next. Making more food. Checking the housekeeper's cleaning skills. (Gosh, did you think I would say I loved to clean? Well, truth be told, I don't mind it, but it's so much nicer to ask for help sometimes.) I would even consider making babies to make food for. This does seem like a way to add stickiness to the value proposition of me having a career by staying home—to care for the micro-humans, and feed them, and watch them grow, much like Chia Pets.

I also love hobbies. I took up tennis lessons recently. I am learning to ride horses, Western style. Next up, I want to learn how to skeet shoot clay pigeons. Not to hunt live animals; I get those pre-butchered for me already at Whole Foods. I just want to target shoot. Calm down, everyone.

It's a novel invention when you can pay a person to teach you a thing and call it "fun." Like I can go out, with my hard-earned money, and trade my money for fun that doesn't always involve public sleeping. What a concept! Please note I still sleep at the beach in regular intervals, mainly because there is no posted sign against snoring.

If I could re-imagine myself, I think I'd choose the career as a homemaker. Just the kind of homemaker that would include enough income for me to fund my hobbies. I think the value exchange is relatively right on point: I have fun and provide food, and in exchange I get to live my life without the pressure of coworkers, calendars, commutes, etc. I think women in my generation were genuinely robbed of this revelation. Or, maybe it was just me. Hard to tell since I prefer to mostly stay home and occasionally pay people like therapists or ranchers to be my fake friends while teaching me real stuff.

The nice thing about a career is that it's not linear, per se. I could decide, today, for example, to become a housewife. I mean, I'm not a wife. There's a slight hitch here in the naming convention when you're unhitched. So I could become a home enjoyer. A lady of the house. A domestic diva of my design. A goddess of my glen. A professor of my possibilities. Would a rose really smell as sweet by the name of "stay-at-homer"? Yes. Yes, it would.

The breadth of a career is really long. I can't imagine committing to one thing for a lifetime. The only thing I can conceive of, and even this is asking a lot, is the ability to reinvent myself. I worry I'll run out of ideas at some point, but there's also a pointless name generator on the Internet so I can come up with a new and bizarre title regularly. Reimagining yourself has a lot of charm. You might worry you don't know how. But you could also generate a random wheel of fortune online and spin it to see what to do next.

The point is, if there is a point at all, the process of reinvention yields the opportunity to not just maximize your potential, but realize it. It also gives you a thing to talk about at family gatherings. "What are you doing?" "I'm reinventing." "To what end?" "I don't know." Then, you can carry around a suggestion box for all your family and friends to put their ideas into and see if anyone comes up with something spectacular. The odds of the answers getting better and better is directly proportional to how much wine is being served. The wine still tastes great, even if it's been aerated in a coffee carafe. I've done miles of research for this book. Truly.

Or, you could concede to the life advice of your college writing professor, Cassie (that's me): "You clearly don't know what you want to do in your life." (True.) "Over the next few years, you might try on a lot of different things, places, and people." (True.) "When you don't know what it is you're meant to do, only then will you discover you are a writer." (True.) "So, just be a writer." (True, but I worry whether it'll stick.)

"Prof C, I love you." And you're right. You were right then, and you're right now. I still have no clue what I'm doing with my life. Writing gives me the outlet to say that sentence in 1,000 different ways. Thank you.

Chapter 5

Let's Worry about Where to Live

Whenever I am applying for an apartment, I don't lead with, "I have lived in seventeen places since the age of seventeen." It doesn't help build credibility as someone who stays and pays. The longest place I have ever lived is the exact home I was brought to after being born... That run lasted precisely seventeen years. Since then, the greatest shelf life I have experienced in any dwelling is two years.

There's obviously plenty to worry about when you move so often, including:

$1 to Change Your Address... And, Why Do We Even Have Mail Anymore?

Telling the world you have moved from one address to another is free, except for when you hit "finish." Then, you need to pay $1 in order to ensure that it is not fraud. Now, I kind of wonder which criminals are out there and have decided to route my mail to themselves. I doubt I'll ever know that they did it, mainly on the account that I never received that mail. I have never been summoned to the jury, so I wonder if this is part of what happened. Maybe someone routed my mail to themselves and then impersonated me as a jury member on a criminal trial. The barrier of entry for this mail switch scheme is fairly low, at only $1. I am really curious which criminals are being deterred by the fee.

A broader question I have whenever I switch mailing addresses for $1 is: why do we even have mail anymore? When was the last time that you received mail that you enjoyed opening, reading, and not immediately tossing into the recycle repository? All of my bills come to me via email. People who I owe money to also have my phone number. I'm not sure why I need a paper trail of... Well, anything at the moment.

Maybe fans will start mailing me letters. I hear hate mail is when you know you've really "made it." Making people mad apparently is a sign of success. I'll keep my address current until I know if that's a thing or not.

Trusting Other People to Pack Your Kitchen

I took a personality test recently to see how much of a control freak I am. It turns out, the test score came back in the fairly low range. I guess that means I either gamed the system or the self-help processes I rigorously employ seem to be working. I can trust people to pack almost anything I own...except my kitchen. Once, I watched someone pack glassware into a plastic trash bag. This was also my ex. And there's a reason why some relationships, like the glasses, become broken. Maybe I'm the kind of person who cares more about my cutlery, linens, platters, dishes, and serving systems more than the average human, but I don't really trust people to pack it on my behalf. I worry others won't be as delicate, dainty, and disciplined as I am when it comes to wrapping each dish, individually, in something other than a flimsy piece of plastic. This is just one area where I don't see giving up control anytime soon, despite the fact that I might have gamed the online test system to decry myself as "not *that* controlling."

Environmental Waste

A.K.A., the whole process of moving amounts to a massive display of paper waste. You have cardboard boxes. Then, you have stuff stuffed into the cardboard boxes like plastic or bubble wrap. Occasionally, you wrap everything in cellophane, like the drawers of your dresser so your socks and underwear don't come toppling out (I mean, who'd waste a box on "unmentionables"?). Between the plastic and paper, there's a tremendous amount of waste generated.

Apparently, there are companies who will rent you plastic tubs so you can make your moving process more environmentally friendly. However, I worry about the sanitation part. Were the plastic bins fully scrubbed in between moves? Did anyone stuff anything unsavory into those bins? What secrets are those bins hiding on their days off?

If I don't go the route of cardboard boxes, I'll miss all the frustrating opportunities to tape things up and slice my fingers open on cardboard, which is a much more substantial paper cut than, say, cutting yourself on thin computer paper. There's nothing to slow down a move quite like a quick slice and a big, bloody mess.

References: Finding Other People to Say Nice Things about You

I have only weaseled my way out of two leases early. And by that, I mean I paid good money to become free from the lease terms, legally speaking. I had good reasons for both, to be sure. But every time I leave a lease, even on a satisfactory note, I worry that the current landlord won't say nice things about me to my next landlord.

It's hard to ask for references. I worry people will go off script. So, I made a policy for myself that I only ask for references while handing people a script of all the nice things to say about me. The conversation usually goes, "Hello, will you please serve as a reference?" Once they agree, I send over a detailed, bullet-pointed list of all the highlights and happy things about me like: pays rent on time, has a sunny disposition, says hello to neighbors, will keep succulents alive but maybe not a whole flower garden, loves dogs but is allergic to cats, would attend a Neighborhood Watch meeting if asked; and most importantly, my favorite hobby is going to bed early and sleeping nine-plus hours a night, so you could say I'm fairly quiet.

Why Is My House Only Clean on Move-Out Day?

The day before move-out day is the cleanest day of my life. My house is sparkling. No surface is left unwiped, untouched, and unpolished. I have made miracles happen in these moments before a final inspection. I worry my house will never be as clean as it is on move-out day.

Why am I only capable of creating cleanliness when there is money on the line? I want to receive that rental deposit back so badly I will literally stay up until 4:00 a.m. cleaning and I am a person who solidly requires eight to nine hours of sleep per night. One move-out, I remember staying up until the wee hours of the morning, scrubbing dirt away from surfaces until my knuckles were cracking open from the cleaning solution, thinking I could buy new hand salve with all the money I'd be saving on my rental deposit return. Someday, I'd like to grow into the person who keeps their house clean for no other reason than it's nice to live in a nice place. Until then, when there is money on the line, I'll be cracking my hands open until the crack of dawn.

Averaging less than one year in a house since I left my childhood home has taught me a lot. I'd like to offer a brief list of what I have learned as being a person who's not necessarily on the run, but hasn't yet mastered the art of staying power.

Here's a few unconventional ways I have made my own moves a little lighter and easier:

Donate All Your Clothes (Except the Ones You're Wearing Right Now)

Moving is a symbol of new beginnings. You can change your address. Why not change your wardrobe? Why not change your name? Change your phone number? Change your friend group? Change your career? I've done all of those at the same time, once, and it is a great way to get a full, clean start. If you want to lighten the load on what to carry over to your next apartment and new life, one easy way to do this is to donate all of your clothes.

I once took my entire wardrobe in a single, plastic duffle bag down to a hip clothing recycle facility that purchased gently used, trendy clothes. I hoped I could sell off my old clothes and fund a new look for my new life. As the salesperson picked up each item of clothing, she did so as if they were dirty, despicable rags. I netted a total of $2 from this adventure for selling precisely two out of about one-hundred items of clothing. She told me in no uncertain terms that they only purchase clothes that are stylish and don't show any signs of wear. I shrugged sheepishly, then broke into a cheeky grin because I knew most of my clothes had come from the thrift store, anyway. I guess there's not a lot of room to run a profit center on buying used clothes, using them more, and then selling them back to a used clothing store.

It didn't actually hurt my feelings that the gal behind the counter told me I wasn't trendy. People have been making fun of how I dress since I was a teenager, telling me I dress like an old person or a mom. But who really doesn't like moms? Everyone has a mom. Moms are generally pretty well-liked. I never saw the issue or felt the sting of an insult with that dig.

I get the pleasure of knowing that I closed out that chapter of my life with an empty closet. I could become anyone I wanted to be next, including someone with slightly more style sense, if the desire arose. One short, ironic trip to the thrift store to drop off all my secondhand, even-more-worn clothes back into the donation pile, I left that life with one suitcase packed and never looked back.

Possessions on the Sidewalk for Passersby

A reasonable person might do something like host a garage sale, wherein they would price their items for sale and net a positive profit from their discarded items. "To some trash, to another treasure," is a popular phrase for upcycled and recycled pieces of a home that once held your life. Perhaps inadvisable from a business perspective, I once set all the items from my house on the sidewalk and told my neighbors they were welcome to have them, take them, sell them, trash them, or leave them for the thrift store donation truck that was coming tomorrow. Seeing their disbelief, I assured them that I was perfectly sane (*a slight stretch, at the time*), and that they were truly welcome to help themselves to the entire contents of my life as positioned on the sidewalk.

I watched as my neighbors scrambled to call friends, grab trucks, and furiously and quickly pack away the contents of my former home into their vehicles. In broken English, one family told me this made their day as they could sell the furniture at the flea market. "Have fun," I told them with a rueful grin.

See, the possessions were all items that had been gifted to me at my wedding years before, back when I had hoped to create a happy home and a healthy life. Back when I had dreams. Back when I thought I needed Pyrex sets, candlesticks, glassware, and picture frames to set up a life that made me feel like a real adult.

I couldn't stand to profit from the pain of letting it all go... So I just let other people—literally—take the load. At that moment, I learned that life can be made up of many things or very few things. I guess much like a person looking back at the end of their lives, you realize you can't take any material items with you.

I still long for a home and a life with holiday china, crisp linens, and vases with which to arrange flowers. But when it's time to nest again, I know the best place to go: the thrift store. That way I can buy gently used, hopefully loved items and recycle someone else's trash into my own treasure. It's like the circle of life for domestic items—what once held hope and created a homey space for someone else can get refreshed and remixed into another, hopefully happier, situation. Someone once told me a thrift store is like a long-term storage facility for which you don't pay rent; similar items will be there for you, again, when you need them. There's something comforting about that.

Rent Only Pre-furnished Apartments

The simplest solution to my ever-shrinking pool of possessions is to only rent furnished apartments from now on. The irony to this plan is that for years now I have been sleeping on beds I don't own and they are far more comfortable than the ones I *did* purchase in discount stores. On the walls are art I didn't curate. But, they're still nice to look at. On the ground are carpets I didn't pick out. But, they're still plush. And the cabinets hold dishes I wash and don't own. But, they still move the food from the plate into my mouth just fine. The genius is that when I need to pick up, move out, and move on, there's very little to carry. There's no telling how long this trend will last, but I've found a winning combo of paying people to design a cozy, little, borrowed life for me and me just showing up to enjoy it. So far, it's been a win for all.

Shower at the Gym from Now On

The best perk about showering at the gym and not at home is that they seem to stock higher quality, more upscale designer soaps than I do. As I've established more and more of a free spirit-type of life of not feeling at home anywhere for too long, I have also released the attachment of needing to use my own bathroom. My bathroom, and I say "mine" loosely since who knows where I'm renting right now or how long it will last, usually contains affordable soaps and towels that I use more than once. When I go to the gym, the accessories are better and I get a fresh towel every time. I only shower after I work out, so I know I have earned the luxury of the little refreshments like a few extra seconds under the hot water I am not paying for. All things considered, I think I might hatch a plan to exclusively shower at the gym from now on—saving me time, money, and water.

Anecdotally, the biggest stressors in life are divorce, bankruptcy (which is the same thing as getting a divorce), changing jobs, and moving. I am pretty sure I should be dead from stress at this point, as I've gotten divorced twice, changed jobs approximately fourteen times (truthfully, I've lost count), and moved seventeen times (as aforementioned). It's hard to keep an account of all the timelines and things when you're so busy living. I used to worry I wouldn't remember all the details, so I've written some down, but I can't find all my notes. Is this what it's like to get older?

The very first apartment I rented as an "adult" was at the age of nineteen. Imagine a run-down hotel turned into apartments in an industrial area of town. To the left, across the street, was a dive bar and a thrift store. To my right, I puckered up next to the train tracks, a tattoo parlor, and an empty lot where trucks would park at creepy hours with strange sounds emerging from them now and again. The decrepit peach paint was flawfully faded, the newly installed roof last century was sagging, and the pavement was so relentlessly unburdened by shade trees you could see heat waves lifting off it in the Southern California summers. When my mom first came to visit, she cried out of fear and pity for me. I'll ink this truth—she wasn't wrong to be afraid.

Signing a lease into this hellishly derelict hamlet felt like a victory for my emerging adulthood and a march toward full independence. And why was I in such a rush to become a fully-pay-my-own-way adult? Mostly so I could eat a non-health store version of macaroni and cheese whenever I pleased (which was all I could afford, anyway). Now I see the value in simply asking your kind parents for money like a sensible teenager. However, nineteen-year-old me had a bone to pick. I needed to *prove* my independence. My path just included a few more frightening moments than I bargained for...

As it turns out, in a seriously dangerous moment, I'm the type of person who's more into flight instead of fight. I blame this on my small stature and sass. Because I'm tiny, it's unlikely I could fight off a bad guy or gal. Because I'm mouthy, it's unlikely I'd be able to hold my tongue and not say something ridiculous that would make things a lot worse in a hostile hostage negotiation. This is mainly why I train for half marathons...so I can run fast, far, and get the heck away.

The day of the shooting started much like any other. Some people in the apartment complex left for work. Some kids went to school. Some people posted up on their front porch like they always did to watch daytime television outside. Some people holed up, like they always did, and watched daytime television inside. I decided to stay in the apartment and work on my homework instead of going to the library at my university.

CRACK. Definitely not fireworks. The shot sounded so close, the paper-thin windows rattled against the molding and cracked wood frames of my study room. Sirens. Cop cars. Police running by my front door, using flashlights to look into everyone's dwellings... And, then there was my response. I did the only sensible thing a gal would do who grew up in a very safe, suburban neighborhood: I grabbed my down blanket and crawled into the bathtub for hours, unable to stop shaking. At least I wasn't shaking from the cold. I think it was ninety degrees outside.

A couple years later, I accidentally landed in an unsafe neighborhood, again. This time, my neighborhood was in downtown Albuquerque, New Mexico. I thought it would be a good idea after college to move to the cheapest place I could find in the continental United States of America, establish residency through hard work, and access bottom-rate tuition prices from a state university. I had just finished my undergraduate degree at a private college in Southern California, so the idea of a lower cost of living and cheaper tuition appealed to me. So much so, that I rented an apartment sight unseen and applied for my doctoral degree. Sadly, only 50% of that sentence contains the truth. I only got to step one: depositing my money toward another defunct dwelling.

As far as stature goes, I'm not a skyscraper. Proudly, on a day after some serious spine stretching, I'm still only 5'2.5". The half is important, to be sure. In this apartment, which I rented with an 'ole-fashioned phone call and a wire transfer that my bank flagged as fraud, I couldn't stand up in the shower. Calling it a "shower" is actually a wild stretch. I was the proud new occupant of a 1920s Victorian home converted into a couple of apartments. I commanded the top floor with a view of crossbars around every window on my home, and everyone else's nearby. The bars provided some sunshade. Inside the bathroom, there was a clawfoot tub. And inside the clawfoot tub there was a shower spout. Sitting down, you would "shower" yourself off like a dog at a posh wash station, and hope that you could hold a little water while scrubbing your wet head at the same time. The ceiling was so short, I couldn't have stood up in the tub if I wanted to. I learned this several half-awake mornings the hard-headed way.

After a small mugging incident later that left me $20 poorer, I decided it was best to stop living next to train stations and transient living facilities. The upside is that the food is usually really good in such areas, and I don't mind a "B" health rating if the "B" stands for "*bountiful* portions" and "*bottom*-out prices." Bill Clinton actually ate at the same breakfast spot in Albuquerque where I enjoyed my weekly indulgence of huevos rancheros, according to the picture on the wall. It's kind of a claim to fame that Bill and I preferred dining in dim-lit breakfast locations with plastic tablecloths and the best freshly made salsa you'll ever have in your life.

Upon their first visit, my parents were confused and confounded by my Victorian apartment victory. These gracious, parental benefactors of mine offered me monetary compensation to remove myself and my belongings from this unit and move to a safer, sounder, more sensible location. I declined. I can't be bribed. You should know that ahead of time in case I am ever installed into a position of authority within a public office—a job that usually requires dual residency with homes in a capital and your district. It's a good thing I'm already prepared to move around a lot.

Next came a very generic, white, bland, new-ish apartment wherein I would watch the sunset over the dusty pink mountains of New Mexico every evening, while eating alone. I would daydream of not eating alone. I learned how to meditate by accident because I focused my attention on one thing and lost track of all other thoughts. I just blankly stared out the window wishing for a different life. A different me. A different dinner. And, I would wonder why the mountains looked pink. I found out it was due to a fungus that only grows at high altitudes in desert climates. This was the stage of life where I found fungus functionally fabulous. It provided the most stunning sunsets, and no, I'm not being facetious or flippant. If you go to the Southwest, you must investigate the fungi twilights in immense detail. There's also nothing else to do there, except go to Walmart on Saturday night and eat dishes made from green chili. I assure you, there will be plenty of time to stop and watch the setting of the big star our planets orbit around which we call the Sun, saying a soft goodnight against the pale, pastel, pink summits.

Sometime later, in my continued commitment to not staying anywhere too long, I shared a 600-square-foot home with my then in-laws. I learned a valuable lesson as a daughter-in-law: whilst humbly accepting help from your relatives, pay for a gym membership and work out every single spare moment of your life. This enabled me to shower at the gym and come home almost never to keep the peace. It worked like a charm, because I was never there to be a nuisance or speak my mind. Plus, I was the fittest I've ever been despite going to aquatic aerobics with the geriatric crowd regularly at 11:00 a.m.

My favorite rental to date came next: another Victorian house split into two dwellings, and again, I secured the top. Sometimes you do get do-overs in life. This was a fabulous one. Compared to bars on the windows in New Mexico, I found myself in this apartment looking at full green trees, lush parks, and eggshell blue skies every day the Los Angeles smog wasn't in bloom. Tucked away into the foothills surrounding the basin of Los Angeles, this picturesque little town was something out of a 1950s sitcom. I had a curmudgeon neighbor who was always mad at me for something, and he hated me so much he ended up buying a mobile home in a 55+ adult community so he never had to hear young people laughing again.

Manicured trees that looked like gumdrops lined my street, and there was faint music playing on the city sidewalks, nondescript and barely audible. I thought I might be involved in a wide social experiment where everyone was part of a suburban simulation— but the plot was so banal and the area so wholesome, there weren't enough moments of intrigue to make up an interesting story.

I have come to miss sleepy bedroom towns from time to time since then. *Boring* has something going for it: predictability. The sidewalks were clean. The streets were routinely swept. The city parks were manicured, and free of vagrants living on the benches. Children actually played outside. Oddly, people could enjoy public parks and spaces. There were no unmarked white vans lingering. Around town, folks would spruce up their homes. Tirelessly, these weekend warriors would keep the paint from peeling and the weeds never won.

I liked suburbia so much, I decided to do the most American thing one could do: buy a home. I wanted so badly to buy my perfect plot in paradise where cops did things like cook pancake breakfasts during community town outings. When it came time to actually procure a home of my very own, I went to the local police station to grill them on crime rate statistics on my exact street. The lady who worked the front desk was exasperated with me after I introduced myself, at age twenty-three, and said I needed to understand the criminology patterns of the fifth safest city in America. She wanted to know what I was trying to find out, specifically. Like a reporter, I told her, "*The truth.*" I spent two hours reading through years' worth of Neighborhood Watch reports and police call logs, just to find out the town was relatively...safe. Boring. Pedestrian. Quiet. Idyllic, even.

I started the home search when I was twenty-two years old. My goal was to buy a home when I was eighteen, and I got laughed out of a mortgage broker's office when I was nineteen. Their disbelief in me was not a deterrent. The steeper the climb on this challenge, the more sassy and determined I became.

I worried that my realtor was going to fire my twenty-two-year-old self as a client during this escapade toward the American dream of homeownership. When we looked at condos, I asked for a detailed report of the finances from the Homeowner's Association; I needed to understand what kind of reserves they were holding, when the last time the roofs were replaced, and what their ten-year improvement plan looked like for the property as a whole. Professionally speaking, I ran this poor soul around and around and around on questions, endlessly. She'd tell me about once a week that no one has ever asked her these types of questions, nor this quantity of questions, let alone a twenty-something first-time homebuyer. I don't mind being the first at things.

So, what happened?

Well, I bought my first (and, so far, only) house at age twenty-three. It was a 1948 bungalow, two bedrooms, one bath. It had a sizable front yard and a bigger backyard. I had zero idea what to worry about until just before the closing time of the home purchase, wherein I had to repair a leaky toilet and a broken fence on my own dime to close the loan to buy the property. "So, you're telling me I have to pay to fix a house I don't own yet?" I asked. Apparently, I did.

Then, the big moment arrived: the key was mine. I remember opening the door for the first time and having a simultaneous sinking feeling about what I did as well as tremendous elation at the prospect of homeownership. It was a profound moment of pride, mixed with a counterbalance of gusto and gratitude that I had made my biggest dream come true.

Peaking early by making your big dreams come true at the age of twenty-three is a really bad idea. It gives you notions that you can do anything. That good things happen in life. That with hard work, grit, and determination, you can make things come to fruition that you have been dreaming about. It gave me a positive bias about myself that I was capable and creative.

But, since most things in life have a counterbalance, I learned that I also could lose everything in one fell swoop.

When I had to put up the house for sale, due to getting a divorce, I called the same realtor who I had only a couple years before almost questioned to death. I simply told her, "We're going to have to sell the house, it's time to liquidate everything." Just like that, the dream was on the market with some perky photos to entice someone else to take the leap and believe in their dreams.

I did one last walk through the home. I touched the floors that I had refinished by hand. I touched the baseboard and case moldings around the doors I had painstakingly measured and learned to install with the help of a patient neighbor who was a real estate do-it-yourself professional. I touched the half-a-century old plaster walls I had painted a cool, calming gray. I touched the terra cotta pots that my mom and I had planted succulents in together. I touched the fence that I painted by hand next to the driveway that I had weeded painstakingly in the blistering summer months. And, with one last touch, I swiped the key and locked away this dream house once and for all.

It's been over a decade since I bought that house. Since then, I have lived in a dark, dingy, soulless studio in downtown Koreatown, Los Angeles. I lived in a chic, modern, sleek, contemporary apartment in mid-city Los Angeles near famous museums and famous restaurants. I've said hello to famous people while they walked down the street to each brunch. I have lived in a glass penthouse overlooking the whole downtown Los Angeles skyline. I've lounged in the pool on the eighteenth floor rooftop deck that was the envy of everyone and home to models, celebrities, and trust-fund party kids. Briefly, I rented a blue-themed flat in Hancock Park, London. I lived in a cozy cottage tucked into the Hollywood Hills, surrounded by secrets and some more celebrities (shhhh, I even lived with one as my landlord).

And you know what?

None of the places I have lived in since buying my house have ever felt like home.

I worry I'll never find my forever home.

So far, I've come to terms with that. I've been doing okay. I've learned home is where your people are. The gym is where the best soaps are. And dishes happen to work just fine as a food vehicle, whether you picked them out or someone else did.

By being less attached to stuff, I've grown to see that experiences are invaluable opportunities to get to know me, and the world around me, better. Especially when the world around me involves a quick trip to a local thrift store, so I can continue purchasing other people's discarded and hopefully previously loved items at a discounted rate. Never pay retail, that's my mantra.

Chapter 6

Let's Worry about Making Friends

Friendship is weird because it's built upon sharing a life with people who like you out of non-obligated choice. In contrast, your family likes you—or pretends to like you around the holidays—out of a genetically obligated choice.

That's just a strange concept if you think about it. We're eight billion souls on a planet with a moon spinning around us as we spin around the Sun, and no one is dizzy. We just live. We exist in a dizzying feat of astrological fervent motion and no one seems to notice. On top of that, we have feelings and emotions and preferences. And somehow, we join up with people who are different from us and not blood-related, and we say, "Hey, let's do fun stuff together because you seem interesting." What an astonishingly bizarre concept.

At my high school graduation, my cousin's husband eloquently told me, "It's all downhill from here." He's a bankruptcy attorney, so he knows. The harsh reality is, after you turn twenty-two and graduate college, you've been put out to friendship pasture. It's difficult to make friends from here on out. If you're reading this and you're under the age of twenty-two, kudos. You still have time.

For starters, here are the best and easiest places to make friends:

At Birthing Class

The most nurturing and nourishing way to form a lifelong friend is not having to form one at all. Outsource this task to your parents. As an embryo, go back in time and ask your parents to choose a really nice birthing class. Find folks who are the salt of the earth and want to do the best they can as parents. These are good seeds for friendship.

So, the best-case scenario is your parents hit it off with some other parents, and you are born into a family friendship that yields you a fellow life journeyer—someone with whom you can share scrapes and scary stories. A playmate. Someone who won't throw a cactus at you because they're mad at you for tattling on them (wait, was this just me?). For the record, I didn't tattle. I was taught not to lie. So, when I was asked a question under oath of not lying due to the wrath of God and parents, I always told the truth. "They're hiding in the cacti plant out back," I said of the missing children. The fact I left out is that I tried to hide with them, but they threw cactus leaves at me. If you are trying to go for friendship gold, go for a more spineless edition. Find friends with a spine. Not cacti with a spine. It's better for everyone involved when you don't have to take out the tweezers to solve a friendship wound.

At the Nursery

If you aren't lucky enough to have ready-made friends following your parent's Lamaze birthing class, then the next more fertile friendship ground would be the nursery. Be it day care, nursery school, or the nursery at your local church, this is an ideal place to swap germs and germinate a friendship. Because at this point you don't have preconceived notions yet of who you are and what you like, you just like to feel good. And you like to play. You are drawn to others who like to feel good and play. This is the easiest time to make friends because you are freed from preferences and checkboxes. Does it feel nice to smash play dough? Yes. Does it feel nice to put things in your mouth and up your nose? Yes. And, no one expects anything from you. If you're a sharing person, and you share the play dough, this will garner you even more friends. Could you jump back in time, you should be more strategic and cunning at this age to use this time wisely to make a best friend or two.

My brother and his best friend met at six months old while wearing diapers. They are in their thirties now and my mom still calls them "diaper buddies." They are as thick as thieves, dress up in coordinating tuxedoes as Lloyd and Harry from *Dumb and Dumber* for Halloween, and enjoy the same sense of humor. But neither of them wear diapers anymore, that I know of. Friendship tip: never share details of incontinence.

At Preschool

I never went to preschool. But I have heard the experience of cubbies is really calming. You're away from home for the first significant stretch of time, and there's a box with your name on it that you're allowed to store stuff in. How much stuff does a toddler really have? I'm not sure. I don't remember being a toddler all that well and I don't remember going places that required me to store stuff at this age. I suppose this could be a really prime time to make friends. You have cubbies with stuff in them. You can trade stuff—if not for friendship, you could make it like a prison gang with different levels of hooch à la Kool Aid or Capri Suns. Alas, kids these days probably aren't allowed to have sugary drinks due to the rise in childhood obesity and diabetes. The more we learn the more we lose, I do suppose. We can collectively scrap this idea as it's a plot filled with more holes than Swiss cheese.

Intermediary Years

People who chose to procreate and then commensurately have miniature humans that resemble them running around the house say things like, "The days are long but the years are short." I guess you could summarize elementary, junior high, and high school as such. Is this a good time to make friends? I would seriously rule out junior high as a good time for anything other than angst, anger, acne, and anxiety. If you pencil in an existential crisis and a bad mood at least once a week, you would be right on track, here.

The benefit to making friends in either elementary school or high school is that you're learning your preferences and how to have distinguishing taste. Discerning between the Backstreet Boys and NSYNC was a delectable debate for me during high school. Other matters, too, arose as a choice of this or that as a way to define my own unique taste and appetite for adventure. For instance, would it be best to visit Nepal or India? I've been to neither but spent an entire summer reading up on Nepal, as I decided Kathmandu would be the better option. I assumed this as a solo quest; however, if I had had a friend to share in this fervor with me, it would have saved me the embarrassment of going to the library, alone, and checking out every book regarding Nepal. The place I frequented most after receiving my driver's license was the public library. And I think even the librarian felt bad for me when she said, "Here again so soon?" in a snarky voice. At this time, I didn't realize librarians were paid public servants. I assumed they were full of snark due to the fact that they volunteered and had to stamp in books all day long and charge fines for people who were late in returning their literature. It was astonishing to realize that you could actually work in a library and receive recompense for it.

Years later, in my early twenties, when I had multiple acquaintances going to school for library science, I had another revelation: apparently there's a science to cataloging books. The world never ceases to amaze me in how many ways we make up fake professions. If you can make friends before you get a fake profession, this seems better. At minimum, you have more time to idle away with pursuits such as checking out every book at the public library about Nepal, and make lists and charts to hang up in your room at home regarding your "research."

At College

College is definitely the preferable, most fertile ground for emerging adult friendship. You're all the same age. Mostly, this means eighteen to twenty-two years old—unless you're a perverse overachiever like me and go from seventeen to twenty and turn twenty-one the day before you graduate college. This is the world's worst day to turn twenty-one because it means I spent the last few years driving every yahoo around as the designated driver, yet no one came to my party because it was on graduation eve.

Suddenly, everyone who spent the last few years yapping about how troublesome their family was was now more than happy to entertain them and miss my twenty-first birthday at a pizza joint. With a rather small rag-tag gathering, I enjoyed sickly sweet shots because I didn't know what else to order.

If you can align the stars to ensure your twenty-first birthday is not the eve before your hopes and dreams come crashing down on graduation day—goodbye to the reality of being a college student and hello working world—please request this ahead of time.

Additionally, if I could go back in time and give myself one piece of advice, it would be this: *don't rush to become an adult.* Don't rush at all. In fact, be lazier. If you told an overachiever they could be lazier, it might mean they're still ahead of the curve but just more relaxed.

Had I been able to take the proverbial "chill pill," I might have ended up picking pineapples in Hawaii or growing coffee in Costa Rica as my career instead of my retirement plan, thus saving me time, money, effort, and confusion along the path of life. I might do that, anyway. Qualifications? Angst and anger, that will help me pick, pick, pick away at the fruit in a gnarly way. Either way, less rush, more plush seems like cush life advice.

Furthermore, college is a fertile friendship ground due to the similarities between all species of collegiate homo sapiens. You eat the same foods. Mostly, this means you all like diner food from Denny's or Norm's wherein you order two eggs over medium, bacon, and pancakes at midnight on a routine basis. You all have the same income. Mostly, this means no income. Unless you're me and you make $85/hour cleaning other people's bathrooms. Apparently this was against the school regulation, but it sure beat an $8 minimum wage by about 10x. (I wasn't even a business major, y'all.) You're all the same level of entitled, educationally privileged emerging adults whilst trying to be art nouveau and angsty. Mostly, this means you have the privilege to sit around and discuss your privilege. Which, I'm just saying for the record, is privilege.

College is participation in a cohort: a group of people who are more similar than dissimilar, moving about life at the same pace toward a similar goal. My goal then was simply to lift my library fines so I could graduate with Latin Honors into the world's worst economic recession. My dreams of the future were succinct: somehow, someway, *someday* I wanted to eat something other than ramen. A decade later, I got paid gobs of money and spent it eating bowls of boutique ramen in the Little Tokyo and Sawtelle neighborhoods of Los Angeles. Everything, it seems, comes full circle. You eat $1 per bag of ramen as a college student. Then you get a career that affords you to buy $50 sake tasting flights and $25 bowls of ramen and think to yourself, "Congrats, I've made it. I have lived the full ramen circle of life."

College is also a moratorium. "Hey kids, enter this moratorium," never caught on as a marketing campaign. But it is one, nonetheless. It's a way to shelter the economy from a mass entrance into the job market flooded by unskilled workers—workers who might earn a reputation for being slightly entitled as they want to know how many breaks they get, how flexible their work schedule is, and what paid holidays they receive before asking how they can provide value on the job. College is great for that type of training—it makes you read the fine print of things and ask the harder questions.

After college, you have a few options of what to do with the friends you have made so far in life:

Stay Friends Forever

Ideally, you age gracefully together and see each other through all of life's seasons. You stand up for each other at your one and only wedding (of course, you might also serve as an attendant for their second or third marriage, no judgment). You will be godparents to each other's children. And when you travel, you make family T-shirts and matching sweatshirts that say something sweet and salty. Your children are friends with one another. You attend your parents' funerals together. And when your spouse-soul-mate passes away, they're the first person you call and cry with. You might even move in for an extended stay. Then, together, you amble slowly around on a nude beach in Jamaica to celebrate your ninetieth birthday. Skydiving for your one-hundredth birthday seems just about the right timing. I'd like to lock in this type of friend in an airtight agreement so they stick with me through all these seasons.

Isn't it strange we share so much of life out of non-obligatory preference with people who owe us nothing? And what if it all goes wrong?

I wish there was a prenup for friendship. You could lay out all the terms of engagement before entering into it, and there's also a clear exit plan. If we break up as friends, who keeps the mutual friends? Whose reputation stays intact? How are we going to split up shared assets and distribute the digital goods like photographs, emails, stories, secrets, etc.?

Stay Friends for at Least a Decade

According to popular science, if you stay friends for ten years, you'll stay friends for life. I read this somewhere once, so it must be true. I guess this is why I stopped talking to my best friend after nine years. I was in pain and didn't know how to say it so I just went off the grid and changed my phone number and stopped talking. My therapist didn't tell me this was unhealthy because I didn't tell my therapist what I'd done. Your therapist is only as good as what you tell them, so if you want your full money's worth, then you should tell them more stuff. This gives them more material, and helps them stay in business.

However, I also play a bit of a cat-and-mouse game. I prefer to see how tricky and insightful the therapist is at getting stuff out of me, which puts us in a lock-step dance of questions and murky answers.

I like to think of myself in therapy like a foggy day, and it's the therapist's job to roll us into sunshine. But if they just nod knowingly at everything I say, it's hard to know if they're really listening or just have their head on a rotating rocking chair of "hmmm" and insert a "tell me more" every now and again.

I've never gone to therapy with a friend, but I think this is an enterprising idea. Hit a rough patch in your friendship? Let's resolve this conflict with a neutral third party. The thing is, if you put in a decade with a friend, you might as well just suck it up and go the lifetime distance. They probably know all your dark, dirty secrets. So, it'd be better to keep them happy and keep their friendship than not.

Stay Friends Long Distance

If you happen to live far away, say, a country or ocean or state away even, it's best to keep up the friendship rather than having to make new friends. Making new friends is super tiring. You put in a lot of effort, like dating, to get to know someone through small talk. Small talk is simply a vehicle to get to juicy talk. But you need to start small because when you lead with something deep, dark, and risky, people tend to run away screaming.

If you maintain a long-distance friendship, it's important to ensure your written communication skills are top notch. A lot can be misinterpreted due to the lack of vocal intonation on written communications like text and email. If you are trying to maintain a cross-continental friendship, you will inevitably rely on written communication since telephones are so last century. The benefit to written communication nowadays is that there are extra characters in which you can ascertain tone and emotionality more clearly than before. These are called emojis. Emojis are emotions represented in cartoon form that convey a sense of feeling that is similar to onomatopoeia (when you say "*zing*" or "*pow*" it is choosing a word that sounds like what you are trying to convey). To keep your emoji game strong, it is essential to choose just the right emoticon to replace the right word. Fluency is key. You do not become proficient at this pigeon language by using the same emoji over and over again. You need to stretch yourself and really expand your vocabulary. If you don't talk to your friend exclusively in emojis at least once in a while, you should question if it is even a real friendship in this century.

Dump All Your Friends

Sometimes you go through a rough patch in life, and as the adage goes, there's only a way through it and not around it. In theory, friendship would lend support during such moments. Some deserts you have to cross alone. Not with a camel. Not with company. Just you and your tears.

During a moment of crisis, one way to eliminate the pain of knowing who your real friends are versus who your poser posse is, is to just unfriend everyone simultaneously. After you have created a clean slate for yourself, you can really get a picture of what type of person you are outside of the influences of your community. This tactic does not garner you a lot of praise. It's actually a bit scary to watch from the outside, I'm sure. But it is occasionally necessary and only to be used in extreme circumstances like joining the circus, method acting preparation by living off the grid, situations of divorce (whereby the clinical classifying term should be "relational death"), or entering witness protection.

Reconnect after an Uncomfortably Long Pause

The aforementioned scenario was not simply a possibility out of my imagination; I actually did some of that de-friending in order to find myself. Nasty business. Both the de-friending and the finding of one's self. My assessment of the process? It was messy, took a long time, and I had to cry a lot. It was just more water than I anticipated. It's easy to get dehydrated when you cry every day, so much and so often that you occasionally can't breathe. And sometimes I would cry until I threw up. Lots of bodily fluid was expelled during this phase, and days were spent in bed like I was an invalid. Once you find yourself emerging from emotional WaterWorld—the place where tears run so freely they flood the landscape of your life—you might want to graciously make amends for your absence.

If you find yourself in the position of the apologizer, it's best to be straightforward and cut to the chase: "I am sorry." While my favorite three words are "you were right" (you thought I was going to say "I love you," didn't you? You sentimental one, you) I have learned "I am sorry" is meaningful and good, too. It's small, short and simple. Like me in real life, standing at 5'2.5" (or about 1.5 meters if that's how people on the metric system measure stature). But really, we forget to use it and we forget to make it matter. If you're sorry all the time about everything, then no one believes you. If you are sincere and self-effacing with your "sorries" then they start to make amends and mean something for someone who might be hurt. Three words can change your life and theirs. So can saying "Go %^&* yourself." But this is a family-friendly book, y'all. And this chapter is on friendship. Those three words won't make you many friends. But they are in your back pocket, just in case things go off the rails. And your mom is out of earshot. Far AF away. (I had to explain what "AF" meant to my mom the other day over brunch. That was unpleasant. Please don't ask me if you don't already know.)

Since the prime time ages for making friends are all under the age of twenty-two, what is one to do when they find themselves wanting to make friends at, say, twenty-three? What about at thirty-three? Forty-three? I shudder. How do you meet your needs for emotional, mental, social, and psychological connection with other humans?

In Cassie-land theory, I think this could easily be solved by taking out an advertisement. For all the dating applications out there in the world, why can't we swipe right or left for friendships? I suppose there could be a way, and, as they say, "There's an app for that."

Here's how my friendship ad would read:

> *Spunky, smart, sophisticated. Loves tennis and horseback riding. In the absence of places to go and people to see, I will dance alone. But dance parties are more fun with at least two people, hence why I'm looking for you. Down for any adventure that isn't illegal, I'm looking to be the Thelma to your Louise without driving off a cliff or ending up dead. If you like copious amounts of wine and cheesy 80s music, we will likely get along well. An idea of a good time together is us getting a massage in adjoining rooms and not talking. What's unsaid is sometimes more important. If*

you take yourself too seriously, I do, too, and I won't hold it against you like other people might. I fight fair if I have to fight at all, but I prefer long-range psychological battles to fist-a-cuffs. Unless we get into a bar fight together, then I'll go down swinging if I really like you and if it's a worthy cause. I'm Irish, after all. If we're just casual friends, I prefer the flight over fight path myself, because I've never been slugged before and I guess it's best to keep just a few things the way they've always been. I don't fear change. I just don't like having to count coins in my hands because they're dirty. Get it? I'm punny. Pleased to meet you.

The thing is, you can't just become friends with plain 'ole anyone. Herein, we've arrived at a crossroads where I should clarify, I have fully subscribed to the *When Harry Met Sally* theory. It is a credo that simply, authoritatively, and unequivocally states that men and women cannot be just friends. I've surveyed many friends on the nature of this theory. Researching this topic vastly—both while inebriated and while sober—I have gone the extra miles involved to expand my knowledge. Even the seeming loopholes— like what if your sexual orientations are different?—have flaws in the foundational argument. I can't tell you why I know without going into too much detail, but trust me. I've researched this. And for once, I think simple is best. And Billy Crystal makes it, if I may, *crystal clear* when he says, as Harry, "Men and women can't be friends because the sex part always gets in the way." Don't shear me with your hairy arguments, take it up with Harry himself.

If you find yourself at the age of twenty-something and ready for a new round of friendships, here are some of the ways you might be able to engage with that type of social behavior, coupled naturally with what to worry about therein:

Therapy

Paying a real someone to be your fake friend is totally possible and it's called therapy. The best part about this friendship is that you never have to host. My therapist had the nicest couch in the best-smelling office with the softest lighting. You get to simply be on the receiving end of the relationship, told how good you are and how far you've come and stuff about you that's nice, warm, and fuzzy. Like the couch cushions. And you get to be deeply listened to. Yes, you have to pay to play. That's the downside; it's not a "real" relationship in that it's not a two-way street. You can't have everything you want at the same time. Sometimes you just have to take what you can get. And incense mixed with instant bonding because they are paid to provide you with unconditional positive regard isn't the worst deal to strike in the universe.

Random Internet Meet-ups

Many, many friends I've made, and only just a few I've kept, I've met off of Internet meet-up sites. This is an insane idea if you think about it. You meet perfect strangers with whom you share one or two hobbies and then you decide, "Let's pay good money to eat out together." Much like dating, the conversation could be banal and you need to get through a requisite amount of small talk before anything truly delicious or delectable can emerge from the conversation. However, if you put in your time, you can start to shine. There's a meet-up for basically everything.

The worst meeting up thingy I ever attended was called "Friends Without Benefits." The premise, which made sense on paper, was that it can be hard for people to meet and mingle while being single. I attended only one event, with many people and many margaritas. Ironically, there were a lot of couples. And a few singles. I was immediately asked out on a date (by a single, I presume) and I never returned, because of the gross violation of the very ideal of the meet-up itself. For the record, I wasn't mad I was asked out. I was mad about the tremendous degradation on the outlet I hoped would be a type of neutral ground—my own friendship Switzerland. A place where I could be friendly without anyone making a forward romantic advance. Referring me back, once again, to the *When Harry Met Sally* theory that men and women cannot be just friends. And, henceforth, I have only attended female exclusive meet-ups. There are statistically less female serial killers. I rest my case.

Book Clubs

Plot summary: these are great. Plot spoiler: they are not about books.

If you fancy yourself as an erudite bibliophile, and want to attend a legitimate outlet for exchanging stimulating intellectual discourse about literature, an Internet book club is not that.

An Internet book club could be rich fodder to meet insane and interesting people, get introduced to edibles, ask inappropriate questions of everyone you meet in the name of scientific research, create political hierarchies based on who gets to pick the book or host the next club, argue over politics with perfect strangers, squabble and create microcosms of in-groups and out-groups, become intoxicated at a stranger's house and driven home by a different stranger (which is better than driving yourself home drunk, I might add), get a lap dance from a stripper, and learn how to give lap dances while drinking shots of tequila. In short, you could find yourself involved with illicit activity in a cult-like environment. It's not clean-cut, family-friendly fun. So now I attend Bible studies, because it's a sane, safe book club and a low-key way to meet other functioning adults. And because it's with a denomination that historically has banned dancing, no one has yet received a lap dance from me. I think we're all okay with that. Everyone has a past. My past just happens to involve a whole will-not-be-written book's worth of activities whilst at a book club.

Walk the Same Route Daily

If you walk the same route in your neighborhood at the same time of day, you are bound to run into (hopefully, not literally) the same people again and again. Whether I was living in London or in Los Angeles, I tried this with some success.

I would see the same people in England hawking newspapers—a difficult road to hoe since there were similar quality-free newspapers right next door—and every day I would say hello. They smiled a type of knowing nod, understanding I was not a paying customer with money, just a smiling neighbor.

In Los Angeles, I would walk the same route daily, see the same folks, and wave vigorously, occasionally shouting hello. I never got to the stage where we exchanged names, because they seemed frightened by my enthusiasm and very existence. If there were a neighborhood for female serial killers to hide out in, I guess it would likely be right where I was in the Hollywood Hills. Buying a T-shirt that says "I'm not a killer" seemed too on the nose. The phrase "kill 'em with kindness" was tough to really apply at scale, due to the fact that no one really wants to die any time in any way, although we all 100% will at some point. I don't use this line to make friends. Not usually, anyway.

Go to Work

There once was a time where work was a place you went to; a physical building with desks and chairs and sometimes kegs of beer and kombucha if you were really lucky. It was a strange time. You arose, dressed in clothes that were not meant for exercise, and commuted by car, bus, or train. You had somewhere to be, so pants were a requirement (unless you were like me and went on a multi-year hiatus from pants and only wore skirts and dresses). You would enter the workplace and spend an inordinate amount of time—sometimes up to twenty minutes—making coffee. Because the commute was stressful, it was stressful to be there, and stressful to have people immediately needing things from you, while caffeine was the numbing agent of choice. The only sane way to hide out and start your day like a real person was to imbibe coffee rapidly by taking as much time to procure it as humanly possible. Some folks had this art down to a science and took forty-five minutes. I could never bring myself to linger that long as a person with a lifelong fear of becoming a blob due to inactivity. *Stay busy. Stay in motion. Stay focused. Or at least, seem busy,* is the mantra of the American workplace.

Once at work, there were humans. Humans who also tried to hide their discomfort with existential feelings of what they were doing there, what their purpose was, and how aligned they were with allocating their time, money, and energy to causes they cared about. There were people who wanted to feel something after years of numbing to fit into a corporate or start-up box (different textures and colors but boxes, nonetheless) that stripped some of their humanity away in the name of profitability and output.

Due to the possibility of collaboration and co-miseration, work is definitely a fertile friendship ground. The problem is, you might find you make friends out of shared complaints rather than anything else, making the extension of this friendship outside of work and into the bars of reality a tenuous possibility. This could get expensive. And it might make you forget for just a moment that good things actually happen in the world. But the communal numbing through alcohol and complaints one evening and coffee with a side of sarcasm to start your day the next morning is one way to get through the experience of going to work. This process is kind of like reading the news: it's an echo chamber for you to better hear your own ideas, drown out any ideas that don't agree with your sensibilities, and feel mildly better that you have the answers and "they" don't.

The other trouble with the process of seeing someone at work and making friends with them is that most digital people don't go to work anymore. We pop open our laptop, making pants, skirts, and dresses even optional. You could go to work in your pajamas, now. It's a bit harder to connect to people when you don't meet them in person, but you have to have mad respect for the people out there who roll up into video chat in their casual loungewear. Nothing says confidence like a sweatsuit on video. I do miss the human connection part. Literally, the talking and the walking, or getting a coffee in person, or happy hour after work that was not in a virtual environment but a very real establishment with four walls and a floor. The world changes in unexpected ways, sometimes faster than lightning and louder than thunder.

Change Jobs

I'm not going to come out and say I'm a quitter, or a job hopper. But people have said this about me. So, here's the thing that no one has thought of: maybe I kept switching jobs not to get a better title, better pay, and a better learning opportunity with more challenges, but rather to procure new human connections in the form of friendship.

I've made some of my very best friends from going to work. I just decided to be friends with them after I quit the job. That way we could know if we were friends in the real world or not. Turns out, we *were* friends in the real world and we never talked about work anymore. This is better for balance but worse for gossip. You win some, you lose some. Having it all is a sham.

Phew. Hopefully you lucked out and have found at least one outlet that works in order to make a decent friend or two. As my dad says, "I had a friend once." One good friend is all you need, really. Once you have a quality friendship, be it one or a few, there's definitely more things to consider.

Here's what to worry about after you've cast the friendship net and are reeling them in:

Should We Travel Together?

Public Service Announcement: Nothing can make or break a friendship faster than traveling together. First, you need to worry about where to go. Then you have to worry about what to do when you get there.

Second, you need to worry about what you'll eat and how often. I knew of a couple of girlfriends who went to Iceland on a micro-trip and drank Coke and ate chips exclusively. I am pretty sure I would die if I attempted such a feat. I mean, literally. Roll me up into a body bag because I'm not coming home if I try to subsist on carbonated sugar and puffed salt for days. Who's going to cook? I'm happy to be the team mom. I'm better than some and not quite as good as others, but I love it. I'm a jolly sous-chef, too. It's the only place I can take authority seriously and listen to directions, because there is mutual benefit to doing it right: everyone wins with a good meal.

Third, you have to worry about pacing. Do you want to do the same activities at the same velocity? Are they going to want to wake up and run on the beach at sunrise or appreciate that I need to sit down and write three pages in my journal before I speak to them? Do they understand the need for nap breaks, or is the pace of adventure going to be so busy that sleep is only for nighttime (which is a scary thought as someone who loves frequent naps on vacation)?

Fourth, are you coordinating outfits? Do you know what you're supposed to wear?

Fifth, does it take one billion years to get ready? I get ready in approximately five minutes flat for just makeup. Yes, the hair might not be done. But I could pull off full hair, makeup, and outfit in thirty minutes or less with a shower involved, so I think I set one of the fastest female records in the history of readiness. What might drive me slightly crazy is if women take hours to get ready. The end result of their lengthy process is not usually that discernibly different from my own accelerated adornment. But I feel like I might die of boredom waiting for them to get ready, and meanwhile might miss all the sightseeing and adventuring.

You need to know these things ahead of time. And this is always—I mean, *always*—why I bring a book. That way I can make up my nose and bury it in a book instead of brooding.

Are We Couple Friends?

It's insanely rare that two humans like each other and become a couple. It's not rare for people to couple up—I just mean it's rare that they really, truly, honestly like each other. It's a sight to behold. Not in a creepy way. Just in a way that I really want to observe it.

Anyway, when the rarity of two people who really like each other come together, it's even rarer that you could find another matching couple who like each other and like you. People who would like you enough to share meals, play games, and possibly go to events like concerts, sporting games, or art openings.

It's a bit of a delicate dance when you like a friend but do not like their significant other. I mean, I try to like everybody, but that is more of a platitude of possibility rather than a reality. The hurtful truth being, of course, that people out there don't like me, either. Ego buster. So, you have to dance this dance with your friends to see if you meet their significant other, and become friends. Will you be friends as a four-person team? What about when you are suddenly single and used to be couple friends? What then? Well, if you're me, you just disappear for a while. I think this is an underrated strategy. Disappear and see who hunts you down. The people who hunt you are probably either 1) stalkers 2) serial killers or 3) real friends.

Can I Call to Cry?

I once wished for better, deeper, truer friendships. Then, suddenly, something strange and unique happened. When I was sad, people offered for me to call them to cry. It was so shocking. "You're saying I don't have to pay a therapist to be my friend anymore?" I mean, I paid a therapist for years to help me learn how to be a better friend, which is obviously a very meta and somewhat perverse joke from the universe because it's expensive. So now I have friends wherein I can ask, "May I please call you to cry?" Or, they text me, "I need a good cry, are you free to listen?" This level of emotionality was something I never prepared for. I worry sometimes it will go away and they'll know I'm ugly crying. But the thing is, just make sure it's not on video... Unless you're pretty crying. There's such a thing as that, too, as someone who has really explored the depths of all the types of tear tracks. Pretty crying is where tears run delicately down your cheeks and you can graciously and slowly wipe them away. The best of friends don't seem to care if you're ugly crying or pretty crying, and they're willing to be there either way. They are so rare and so precious, I want to wrap them into bubble wrap and hide them away for safekeeping. I mean, as a metaphor, of course.

Who Pays the Bill?

Nothing is more worrisome to the health of a friendship than someone who keeps a tally on which friend owes what exact amount on the dining out bill. If you have three guests, split it three ways. Now, if I am the resident alcoholic, and I order a brunch cocktail when no one else does, I should cover the whole tip. There's always a smart and rational way to divvy up the bill without itemizing it. I have run away from more than one friendship when they sought to itemize the bill for a group dining ticket. I can't abide. First of all, it's just too much math when I'm out and about trying to enjoy my life. Second, I probably had a drink, so I really don't want to do math right now. Third, men don't do this. I ask them a lot. They just split the check based on how many bodies were there and don't give a care.

Finally, the best-case scenario is that you're financially abundant enough to pick up the check... Or let someone pick it up for you. This reciprocity and generosity is a really good sign for friendship. Sometimes I'm the friend that picks up the expensive meal check. Sometimes I'm the friend who will help you hide alcohol in a can of soda while listening to sidewalk jazz. I'm good in a creative pinch.

How Good of Friends Are We?

In dating, there comes a time to define what we are, become exclusive, and name it and claim it: we're girlfriend/boyfriend now. In friendship, the way this happens might be more meandering but eventually you need to name the friendship somehow. Are we casual? Are we exclusive? Are we a cult? Should we start our own church so we can have a tax shelter? Are there rules? There are just a few boundaries. Sometimes "best friend" isn't the right term. So you find a soul sister. Sisterhood is even next level. Once those words are spoken, the vows are invoked. When someone tells you that you are their best friend, or soul sister, it means something. It's a ride or die commitment now, but I don't want to have to go to jail for anything on your behalf if I can avoid it. It'd have to be for a very, *very* good cause. One "very" isn't enough in this instance.

Can You Take My Picture?

The best and most real test of friendship is how well they take your picture. If you are comfortable with them taking your picture, your smile will shine and you will beam your stardust magic into the world like never before.

Real friends will go the extra mile to take a thousand angles, tell you where to put your eyes, how to pose, and what emotion to exude. They will take picture after picture after picture to make sure you look just right in the lighting. And they won't complain. They do this because they like you. And they'll tell you how to edit it and which one is the best for your future online dating profile you don't intend to create. And then they'll feed you after the photo. Because life isn't about posing or stunting, it's about living and eating. And telling stories. And laughing until you can't speak.

And what do you do to *keep* your friends? If you've spent all this time, effort, money, and sweat equity to invest in a relationship, how the heck do you maintain it?

My mom has an average tenure of friendship of thirty-plus years. Some of her friendships span fifty years. This is unfathomable to me. But in the name of research, I've tried to study these people and why they still like each other.

Here's what I came up with that will make a friendship last:

Laughter

I think humor is the best thing to share. If you don't have a similar sense of humor, you should just end the conversation mid-sentence, pay your half of the bill, and run away...from a friendship. From the bar. From a date. From anyone. If you can't laugh at the same things, you'll probably cry about different things. And then this is a bunch of messy emotions bound to erode the friendship in all ways. Just cut your loss if the laughter track is switched to "off" when you tell your best joke. Trust me. A lot of people have run away from me in my lifetime. I bless the mess they leave. And I obviously finish their leftovers. I'm a glutton for food if not for punishment.

Shared Love of Food

I'm most likely to be friends with people who share breakfast with me and then talk about lunch. At lunch, we wonder about dinner. And at dinner we discuss the whole day's meals ahead.

One casual acquaintance once asked me, "Tell me everything you ate today." I thought I found a friend for life but accidentally deleted her phone number and she moved across the country and I lost touch. But, it had the making of a lifelong love affair over what we ate recently.

Abundant friendship is built around delectable food. Eating food. Talking about food. Making food together. If you don't like the same foods, you might as well cash in your chips and just guzzle the guac with a spoon.

Pacing

Friendships, like the ocean tides, have a natural ebb and flow. If you are a person who loves to walk with their friends and often engages in walking and talking, it helps to have someone who literally goes at the same pace. My mom naturally walks a ten- to thirteen-minute mile. Except with me, when she walks a fifteen-minute mile. She'll walk even faster when she's angry. Because a ten-minute mile for me is an accomplished slow jog, I didn't think it was really possible for her to find a friend who matched this insane pace. I'm (almost) always happy to be proven wrong (if it's for a good cause). One day, I saw my mom and her friend discussing politics and solving world problems while walking an under-thirteen-minute mile. And I thought to myself, *Friendships that thrive know how to jive.* And pace. Pace yourself. Pace your friendships. Pace your literal steps. This seems to be a key ingredient in healthy friendships.

Time-Outs

Sometimes you just need a break. Friendships that are elastic and flexible and loving and kind know this and provide you with lots of breathing room. Don't want to talk to me for a couple weeks? Cool. Just let me know. I'll be around.

I feel immensely fortunate to have people who love me enough to say, "I'll be back," and actually mean it. And who give me the space to do the same. It's not unusual for my friends to receive a text stating, "I can't talk right now because I'm having a scheduled existential meltdown."

Similar Life Stages

It seems that people are more compassionate about canceling plans at the last minute if you tell them the truth about why you're bailing. For example, "I have an unplanned existential crisis today," lands well with people who also don't understand what they're doing with their life.

People also tend to understand when you say, "I can't talk or hang out today because I'm taking the whole day to cry," if they also went through a traumatic breakup. So, it's good to have friends who've broken up and made up and moved on and all the in-betweens. More experiences mean more things to talk about.

If I am spending all my weekends pretending I am on an HGTV fixer-upper show and going to Home Depot like it's a social destination, and other friends are also remodeling their new houses, we have common ground and can swap sweat hours. Actually, I did this, and it worked fabulously to save money on tools.

Finding people who are in a similar life stage and have a similar bank of experiences just helps solidify things.

Values

Betty White is obviously the most golden of the girls. Old movies are better than new movies. Music with instruments is better to dance to than electontrica. The 1970s produced the best music of any decade, ever, hands down, bar none. Kids shouldn't go hungry. Literacy should be available to everyone. Public libraries should continue to receive funding. And reading aloud with people you love is better than watching television together. Aligned values are what build lasting relationships of any kind. Share the values, share the life, I say.

I guess you learn the value of friendship from the first friends you have on this planet: your parents.

Like I told you earlier, my dad always tells me, "I had a friend once." And, he's the most likable guy you'll ever meet. There's no shortage to his affability. He's just an introvert who prefers to stay home, grill on the BBQ, and be cozy. He doesn't find it all that thrilling to meet perfect strangers and have perfectly deep conversations with people he doesn't really know. (I, personally, find befriending strangers a sport.) He's taught me the value of being slow, methodical, and choosy when making friends.

My mom, on the other hand, strongly believes that every friend is your best friend. She tells me this every time I get a new "best friend." She talks to strangers. She taught me that there's no such thing as strangers—everyone is just a friend you haven't met yet—which is probably why I feel perfectly comfortable going into a bar, alone, and singing karaoke. The whole bar is cheering me on and secretly they want to be my friend, right?

If you want the very best friend in the world, you should meet my mom. You probably can't meet her and won't meet her, but my mom would be your best friend. She is enthusiastic, down for any adventure, and loves to try new things. She's loyal. She loves your stories. She'll laugh at all of your jokes. She means what she says and says what she means. She is mighty. And feisty, too. And she'll literally tear up a rug or lawn depending on the dance venue.

I wish when I grow up I could be just like her. I look like a dead ringer for her, just thirty years apart. So when I introduce myself to people who know her but not me, I say that I'm her mini-me, just taller. She's also my best friend, too.

I hope you get as lucky as me someday. You can't recruit *my mom* to be your best friend—that would be too easy. Plus, she's taken. My mom is busy being my best friend because I'm a handful, like a latte...just a tad more than a cappuccino, really. But hopefully I gave you a picture of what's possible in friendship. My mom says hi, by the way. (And she's the reason I wrote this whole gosh-darn book. So either I'm sorry or you're welcome, Mom.)

Chapter 7

Let's Worry about Being Best Friends with a Celebrity

Take a brief moment, as if we're at a baseball game, to stand up and do the seventh inning stretch. We've made it through the worry wilderness thus far. Of course, there's more terrain to trek. And more things to worry about and inspect. It rhymes, and we've got nothing but time. So sit back after stretching and allow your muscles to relax. You've spent enough life energy already paying the worry tax.

There's a really good chance that many people will read this and call it dreadful drivel. There's a wildly off chance someone who is already a famous tastemaker and commander of comedy might read this book and actually like it. And because I'm curious about the things which have a low likelihood of occurring, as any good worrier should be, I'm going to focus my attention on the latter.

What if a celebrity becomes your best friend? How would your life change?

I'm not sure how this worry originated. But it dredges up a lot of concerns about friendship in general, and of course, specific questions, too. For example, do you befriend the bodyguard, too? Are you allowed to open your own car door handle if you're being chauffeured around? How do you deal with paparazzi? What is the nature of existence?

The first thing that would need to be established is how we are allowed to talk about this friendship. It is a really powerful move in any circumstance to become friends with someone and have them sign a legal non-disclosure agreement. I'm sure the famousness of the person in question would ratchet this up significantly. I've thought about typing out an NDA for my friends and family to sign in the off chance I might become a famous friend myself. It sets a precedent to lock everyone up in secrecy long, long before then.

A list of questions for your future celebrity best friend: are we allowed to discuss our friendship on social media? How should I refer to you? Do you prefer Ma'am or Ms.? (As aforementioned, I don't have male friends.) Should I run my social media posts by your Public Relations people? If we're taking our relationship to this level already, should my people talk to your people?

If I don't have "people" at this stage of the game, I'd hire my brother who is fabulous at impersonations and accents. I'll have him talk about my image and how important it is to preserve it, mainly to ensure my newly minted celebrity best friend should not appear in a way that's offensive to my belief system. Offensive, say, like eating Chick-fil-A on a Sunday. Maybe my BFF owns the chain and opens up the kitchen for private tastings that day only, and doesn't invite me. This is bad for their image and mine because if you are real friends and want perks, like gosh-darn good chicken on a Sunday, you need to sneak me in, too. I'd put this in our friendship contract, specifically, on its own line item. I crave Chick-fil-A mostly on Sundays.

The other thing I would want disclosed before the friendship deepens is an exhaustive list of mutual connections in finance, economics, business, and government in case we're at lunch with them and I happen to hear stock tips dropped over the meal. The last thing I need right now or ever is getting involved in insider trading. I'm unsure if insider trading could be considered a crime if women ran the world because we rarely operate any large decisions without consulting a consortium of trusted folks, vetted folks, family folks, friend folks, and maybe even random strangers for survey purposes. It's hard to know at the end of the day where I get my own information sometimes—attribution can be really tricky. But the last thing I want to do is accidentally end up in jail due to insider trading. I accidentally got married and ended up in divorce court, and that's sobering enough to keep me on the straight and narrow forever.

Being a celebrity, there's likely a strict diet to follow based on upcoming roles, red carpets, and other public appearances. When I eat breakfast, I think about lunch. When I eat lunch, I'm thinking about dinner. And after dinner, I think about the entire day of eating ahead. I have plenty of time to do this since I do intermittent fasting, and only eat food between eight hours of the 24-hour sun circus. With my celebrity best friend, I'd want to know ahead of time what we're eating. If they're on a strict diet, do I need to pack a peanut butter and jelly sandwich to go to Malibu Beach for the day? "Will I go hungry?" is usually my number one question for any trip, long, short, or even a quick jaunt to the gas station. I think getting this sorted right out of the gate by getting a run-down on their allergies, preferences, no-go foods, and calorie intake would be easiest and most suitable for all involved. I'd do this for pedestrian friendships, too. "Nice to meet you, tell me everything you ate today," is one of my preferred lines for opening up a new connection to light conversation on meaty topics.

While we're at it, I'm not sure why someone hasn't invented a dating application that matches people up based on what they're currently eating and what they aspire to eat. I could swipe left or right in the In-N-Out line based on people who don't order off of the secret menu. Don't you even know about Animal Style? If you haven't discovered this by now, and you live in California, we're probably not a match because you're not adventurous enough. Plus, it's a real turn-on to push the rules, find the secret menu, and wonder what else is possible in infinitesimal combinations of what to do with fried onions and Thousand Island spread. If you can't mine the secret menu at In-N-Out, how could you possibly mine my mind for information?

The flip-side is that I want to know if someone has good

judgment, like, "I'm going to eat Animal Style fries for dinner but I know I should be eating grilled chicken and asparagus." At least I know they are capable of making a choice and sticking to it, even if it's the wrong choice. I wish in life that there were points for sticking out bad decisions. My quitting record goes down if you average out the number of my bad decisions by the proportionate amount of time I spent suffering the consequences bravely. Somehow, I've never received a medal or trophy for this, it's just a private badge of honor I would possibly disclose in the deep recess of truth-telling, like on a dating app based on food preferences.

Next, we need to discuss our socialization strategy. Is it appropriate for me to go as your plus one to a party, celebrity best friend? If so, what do I need to worry about? Am I allowed to make eye contact with other people at the party? Or is that above my paygrade on the social stratification level?

One friend drilled into me the importance of never looking impressed around well-to-do people. Maybe you now realize I've come from salt of the earth stock, but I don't have much experience acting unimpressed around impressive people. Of course, who defines "impressive," right? In those scenarios, I imagine adopting a blank stare and nodding knowingly, to anything and everything, rather than smile too wide and slightly lopsided like I normally do.

The thing with friends is that you typically adopt some similar habits, perhaps likely shared activities and likely similar foods eaten within the span of eight hours, as previously discussed. I'm curious if this celebrity friendship comes with a dress code. I was once out to dinner at a five-star hotel in Santa Monica, California with some people who fancied themselves as fancy folks. Not celebrities, but richer than average, to say the least. Upon entrance, I got "oh's" and "aw's" about my emerald green dress with a jungle frond and tropical floral print. "Where did you get that dress?" Like the 90s commercial jingle, I said in a sing-songy voice, "I got it at Ross." Their jaws dropped. Their designer wear seemed to crinkle faster than their faces wrinkled in both dismay and envy.

When I was young, I didn't know it was impolite in certain

casual company to return a compliment about your fashion choices with a financial rundown. "Hey Cassie, love your top," is a phrase I would return with an enthusiastic commercial, "Wow, I love it too, and best yet, it only cost $5.99 at Ross." I have been pushing people to my favorite store for years, unprovoked and unmonetized. I was later informed by my then boss's boss that I discuss the thriftiness of my acquisitions like others brag about their designer or name brands, thus further cementing the immutable law that we're just all lovely humans on a spectrum of spending. My league's coat of arms simply reads: "Thou Shalt Never Pay Retail."

One of the best things about being a celebrity is getting endorsement deals. The endorsement I would most love to secure is being the lifetime spokeswoman for Ross Dress for Less. Then, I could receive first access to designer wear at a discount, and proudly proclaim every time I walk into a room, "I got it at Ross." My future children would be outfitted, my patio spic and span, and my throw pillows fluffed. Let alone all the matching luggage I could buy for my whole future family to fly in style. If I am ever invited to a lifestyle magazine photoshoot, I will let the booking agent know I will graciously accept the gig only under the specification that all gear must come from Ross due to my sponsorship deal.

Another troublesome aspect of friendship and fame is: what if one of your current friends becomes famous? Imagine you've been besties for years. You brunch. Even when it's basic. You lunch. Even though you just ate brunch. You crunch the same granola and wear the same brand of athleisure to Whole Foods. You have a pose set for your selfies and you know exactly how to edit them to your friend's preference on black point, contrast, and brightness. True friendship is filtered selfies.

Then, suddenly, after years of blood, sweat, tears, and auditions, they hit it big time. Mega famous. Do you stay friends? They can't have lunch after brunch anymore because they are on a diet regime for the next film cycle. They can't wear athleisure to Whole Foods anymore because they have a person who picks up their groceries. (Oh shoot, that's just called Instacart and you don't have to be insta-famous anymore to have groceries delivered for a low,

low rate.) Selfies are out unless they're authorized by the freshly established Public Relations team. In which case, I suppose I'd try to leech some free advice about my Instagram feed and see if they think I should punch it up more with jokes or be more dark and moody to evoke real, deep emotionality. You have to sign an NDA to say you won't disclose the details of your relationship, which we already covered is a good idea up front and regardless (pauses writing, gets out to-do list and tacks this on ahead of the book release).

The point is, what is a friendship over time? How do you move together with the seasons of life if you're no longer in the same stratosphere? Does someone being well loved in public still want to be well loved in private?

I worry it might make my clout as a friend go up in an uncomfortable way if I were the friend that became famous. People might want to be my friend just because I'm "someone." But the thing is, we're all some-bodies to some-one, somewhere.

The best thing about being best friends with a celebrity would be getting driven around. I'm not talking about a car-sharing service. I mean, a certified-safe bodyguard driver. I'd never have to worry about directions, getting the gate code, remembering the gate code, or opening my own door. I hate driving so much on any given day I would rather pay someone to take me around, anyway. But this friendship would guarantee I would not be allowed to willy-nilly input the directions into Google Maps while fiddling with Pandora on the radio instead of Spotify, which is what the cool kids use. I would no longer have to wear a necklace of garlic to ward off road rage and other bad spirits that possess you out of anger on the 405 Los Angeles freeway to hell. And I wouldn't have to pray that the guardian angels would prevent an accident. I forgot to do that the other day on the way to work, only a fifteen-minute drive, and almost got into two accidents. The thing is, my celebrity best friend's life is worth more than mine, from a profit and loss standpoint. So the biggest perk is that the precious cargo of life would be carted around in true luxury, also known as simply employing a driver.

While out and about with our driver, drinking smoothies and

going to expensive barre ballet fitness classes, it's possible we'd run into the paparazzi. And I'd get credited as an "unknown friend." This, everyone, is much better than a compliment.

It's the most uncomfortable experience for me to have an unprovoked nice thing stated to my face. I have to assume I'm not alone. But if I am, then don't email me to rub it in.

The worst experience someone could give me is to say something nice. *Cringe.* I have a visceral reaction against niceties. I'd rather discuss the weather at length and high-pressure systems with low-pressure movement than to hear I did something well. I feel obligated to downplay it. To make sure I don't accept compliments graciously, I have a battery of responses ready like:

- "Okay, thanks, but it was easy, anyone could've done it."
- "It was luck."
- "It was a coincidence."
- "It was because of a genetic abnormality. I was born this way, and it's no big deal."

It does not seem appropriate to come out and say, "Well, I know it looked effortless and smooth but I put in eleven years of work and dogmatic swings of self-abuse and positive affirmations to get here after the $10,000 I spent in therapy." No one wants to hear the truth about how I did something impressive and all the sweatiness that went into it—at least that's the story in my head.

I wish there was a forum where we could compare notes on how we got from point A to point B without a competition, if it wasn't bragging to say things exactly how they were. Like, "I spent the greater part of the last ten years reading about finance and that's how I made my first $1,000,000 while day trading over the last ninety days." I mean, that's not *my story.* But I suppose it could be someone's. And they would likely sell this story in the form of a course and a coaching package to teach you to do the same. "But there's an element of bragging," those of us on the outside might say. What's the line between self-promotion because you own a business and bragging about your own accomplishments simply by telling the truth of how it happened?

Because of the interwebs, we all have a greater likelihood of becoming famous and/or becoming millionaires. The latter is largely impacted by inflation and the rise of digital business options, but is true even so. So it's almost just as possible you could become a famous friend to someone else as it is that you could become friends with someone who is famous.

I worry the goal post is about how others see us and not about how we see ourselves, here. That if we have the greatest following online, make the most money, have the objectively best body (by whose standards?), then we will have "made it." Then we can be happy. Then we can have the friends we want (famous or not). Then we can attract the romantic relationship of our dreams.

I worry about the "then" trap. *Then*, I will be happy. Then, I will travel. Then, I will quit my job and live my dreams.

So I just chose to up and do it one day. I quit my job. Quit my marriage. Quit Los Angeles. Heck, I quit the United States. I moved abroad. And I was greeted, almost momentarily, by a pandemic.

The thing is, when you take a risk and make *today the day*, it doesn't always go your way. Or, the way you planned. It isn't always a success story by outside measures. You might not get famous or fit or fabulous. I got two out of three, so I'm batting a pretty good average. I'll let you guess which ones.

The point is, "then" is really never.

Let's do a quick thought experiment. Just replace "then" with "*never*": *I will never be happy. I will never travel. I will never quit my job. I will never have a happy relationship.*

And choose what path you want. Choose then, which is really choosing never, or choose when you will get started. Choose to decide if "never" is true for you. Will you be okay with never doing it? Never living your dreams? Never trying?

Choose your own adventure. Choose when. Make it happen. If you can't just commit to it fully, commit to trying it out.

If you follow this then -> when formula (trademarking as we speak) and make real, substantial, unequivocally authentic changes, I've just saved you $10,000 in therapy and years of inner self work.

Chapter 8

Let's Worry about Getting a Massage in Another Culture

Massage is pretty great because it's a legal way to get people to touch you in appropriate ways. For someone who experiences the world through touch, and despite all appearances is actually an extrovert, the COVID-19 pandemic was like a touch-deprivation chamber. I couldn't hug people. I couldn't touch random dogs on the street to say hello. I couldn't share the sidewalk; people saw my freaky 5'2.5" frame and jumped out of my way like I was a bulldozer with a spear on the end of it. Most people were even against elbow or fist bumping, which was kind of like a missed opportunity to have an arms-only, micro dance party. It was a very confusing time for me and my physical touch-y-ness.

If we rewind the movie (remember when that was actually a thing?), I have to admit that it took me a while to find my massage stride. I tried many, many places. Or, really, they tried me. They tried to fix me, break me, and patch me back together. I really think anyone who's ever given me a massage probably called their massage instructor and said, "You won't believe who I just met—a girl who looks totally normal at age twenty-something and has the back of a sixty-something-year-old." Or, I can just hear the masseur muttering under their breath, "We've done all we can, we just have to see if she's going to pull through."

A lifetime of worry created a lifetime backache. I'm my own

literal pain in the ass.

I started my massage journey when I started making money. I was stressed at work, so I figured I should pay to de-stress. I worked eight hours (joking, I always worked more) every day during the work week, then spa-d it out for at least eight hours on the weekend. This was my working plan for a couple of years. It worked, until the world shut down and no one could legally touch me for a while.

It all began at a chandelier-dripped-in-crystal type of place in West Hollywood, California, home of movie stars, restaurants, bars—and spas—that would gladly help you drown your work sorrows away while separating you from the money you worked hard to make. Bourgeois, upper-class massages at places of comfort are wonderful, if not outrageously priced. Any upper-scale spa in Southern California provides everything you could imagine wanting from a spa visit: sumptuous robes, crisp towels, spa shoes that don't quite fit a size 6.5 woman's foot (which, according to most of my friends is child size), luxurious pools, saunas, hot tubs, steam rooms, a nap room which they call a "reading room," a breezy lounge, a blow-dry bar, a nail salon, a storefront for your skincare needs, and even an apothecary on site to mix you the right aromatic blend of massage oil for an extra $25 on your already $200 spa visit.

The strangest thing about an invite to spend a day at a spa such as I have described for you, dear reader, is that they don't sell food. They want you to buy the apothecary's upsell, and spend a few hundred dollars more on skincare products that you received during your facial treatment. But in the process of asking me to spend $500 or more per visit, there's also upsells, cross-sells, and just sales. Meanwhile, when I went to this serene, lavish, extravagant spa, they forgot to sell me a smoothie, a cold-pressed juice, or a granola bar. I really would have been okay with an upscale vending machine if it meant I could spa + snack. Actually, maybe that's a new spa-chain franchise concept: Spa+Snack. (Trademarks it online.)

Honestly, when I spend even *just a measly* $200 on a spa day, I want to get my money's worth in terms of hours spent relaxing.

If the median household income is $55,000 in America, that's about $211 per day in income. If I'm planning to spend what a median family's daily income is at a luxurious day spa, then I expect to spend at least four hours or more getting all the free lemon cucumber water, bananas, tea, and waxy apples I can get. I want to go the distance, and spend as much time napping in the semi-public spaces as possible, but I'm famished. No one has proposed the idea of integrating food into the experience of spending all your disposable income on services that are counted in minutes. We exchange our hard-earned money in the strangest ways, sometimes.

I could have stopped there, and thought, *This is the pinnacle. I can spend all my money on things I don't need, when pining about how to get the sustenance I crave* (which is not love or drugs, just to be clear. It's food). I could have succumbed to a spa life of waxy apples and under-ripe bananas that adorn the water station. (And, honestly, I'm not even sure they're meant to be eaten or just admired from a distance.) But aren't humans mostly still animals, anyway? Maybe the waxy apples are a trap to see if you come from blue-collar blood, where you feel you must eat everything at the buffet to get your money's worth. Secretly, the skinny, upper-class waifs are snickering at you consuming the still life art arrangement.

I like to think of myself as the remaining vestige of the soon-to-be-erased middle class—an enterprising capitalist who would just install a damn fine but damn overpriced juice bar in the lobby. And I'd definitely upsell swirled chia seeds into your smoothie. Nothing gets stuck in your teeth like a chia seed. Unless you've paired it with raspberries. You should just schedule your dental cleaning ahead of time if you're planning to eat this combination. That's called *adulting* at its finest—thinking ahead for dental cleanings based on your meal planning. I mean, I already make most of my life decisions based on meal plans. Might as well throw my dental calendar in along with the fun. Isn't that the point of getting older? Finding the fun in dental scheduling?

While they see me eating art, I see making a large profit margin on the sneers of skinny people looking to go on a liquid diet. Maybe this is what makes America great. We each have dreams about eating waxy apples, or juicing the same waxy apples for profit.

Spoiler alert: this initial foray into fancy, fine spa-ing wasn't the be-all end-all for me. I soon learned that in living in a densely populated, diverse city, there are a lot of cultures offering a massage getaway escape. Probably, there's a coupon for it on an Internet daily deals site for about 66% off retail price. You might buy it, but you'll likely never redeem it. This is how they make profits—on you not using the stuff you bought. Genius, right?

The trouble is, there are things to worry about when getting a massage in another culture. Like, what if there is a language barrier and you can't say, "The pressure is too intense due to my lymphatic drainage cycle combined with the way my bowel movements have changed from my kale juice diet, so if you could ease up ever so slightly on the pressure in my mid-lumbar region, that would be so appreciated." Some things just don't translate well across cultures.

I fancy myself as a massage ethnographer, and it's a bit murky still if I can write off the multiple visits to the Korean spa as "research." But it is just that: research. I just happen to have a fascinating, and immensely relaxing and gratifying discipline of study. This is America. You can be a massage researcher if you want to be. Maybe I'll log 10,000 hours in massage treatments before I'll allow you to deem me an expert. Filing this idea away for a future New Year's resolution I really don't want to make and yet hate to break.

So, after scrupulous hours putting myself in the line of duty to research massage options cross-culturally, here are the things you need to worry about if you choose to get a massage in another culture. It's a choice I would highly recommend you try, too, after the commiserate amount of worrying, naturally.

Chinese Foot Spa

My very first trip to a $15-per-hour reflexology foot spa was at a place called something like Master Wong's. It's so long ago; details fade into the horizon of a smoggy Los Angeles sunset. The scene is circa 2011-ish. I can't remember dates as well as my mom, and since she wasn't there, this will have to suffice in accuracy. I set my GPS for somewhere I've never been, which, in Los Angeles, is usually the case. I arrived at a derelict strip mall with my childhood best friend in tow.

Primarily, she agreed to attend because I said I would pay. Bribes are so beneficial. The asphalt was torn up, with paint lines to mark parking spaces that were peeling, which set the stage for a shopping mall constructed sometime in the 1980s and had been unloved ever since. The roofing sagged, everything was painted a certain hue of brown that resembled scorched earth, and about 50% of the retail stores were closed or out-of-business. *Perfect.*

We walked into Master Wong's, following the yellow lettering on the front door. My college professor swore by this place and said it was the greatest treat you could ever give yourself. She was also a writer, so it's hard to tell if this was embellishment on the scale of hyperbole, sarcasm in the form of a perverse joke, or evangelism seeking to enlighten my senses and expand my horizons.

I read the sign: $15 for a one-hour foot massage. "Two of those, please." We were ushered to sit in recliners that might have been purchased from a thrift store last decade, but there was a (hopefully) clean beach towel between me and the chip grease from that one Super Bowl where John Elway played. I sat. My friend was eyeballing me and communicating just plenty without words. I ignored her. "This will be great," I smiled. She was not reassured. I wasn't sure, either, but I was committed. Sometimes that's enough.

The recliner I was in was next to the recliner my friend was in, which was next to about twenty other random humans. We were all in one room with no curtains in between us. Everyone was clothed. It was somewhat reassuring to be touched by strangers in the presence of other strangers watching you. And I hoped there were a few moms in the crowd who would yell in case anything got out of hand.

My feet were plucked up from under me and submerged into boiling hot water. I turned lobster red immediately and felt like I might accidentally pee my pants. I didn't, just for the record. A washcloth was placed over my face. If this was a Liam Neesen movie, I'd bet this is the point where I am kidnapped. My senses were dulled, my inhibitions lowered as the water temperature cooled and I no longer felt my flesh was roasting and falling off the bone. I was just relaxed enough to sink a tad deeper into my defined, dented recliner, and forgot for just a moment that I was in a fishbowl of flesh with other humans about to be vigorously massaged like a kale salad.

And as unceremoniously as my feet were submerged, the massage commenced. "Man-handled" might be a better word to describe this. The man took my neck and knots and pulverized them. I engaged in deep, labor-style breathing. I'm not a mom, I've just watched a lot of movies in my Human Growth and Development Psychology class on the magic of birth. I believe he muttered something like, "Too tense," under his breath. I know I looked too young to be that stressed out, but he didn't know about my lifetime achievement award in worrying and how to dissect all good out of your life through generalized concern.

It felt like a combination of a rub and being slapped with a meat tenderizer. I peeked beneath my washcloth to ensure my bestie had not been abducted. She looked distinctly unamused. I wasn't sure if we should have asked for less pressure. I wasn't sure we *could* ask for anything other than what we were being given—so I attempted to switch myself into this uncomfortable, out-of-my-comfort-zone thing called "receiving mode." This is the mode, unused in my life, wherein I just receive what happens to me with grace and aplomb. *Let's see what happens next*, I mentally "texted" my best friend, with my warm, knowing smile, as if I somehow trusted we'd make it out in one piece.

Eventually, the men stood up to take away the foot water, which had gone cold. I looked at the clock; it had not been an hour. But they did not return. I peered suspiciously around my washcloth, not wanting to make waves. But I wanted to get my full $15 worth per person, thank you very much.

Our masseurs were outside smoking. *Cigarettes between cellular massage therapy.* They returned. I had questions. I left said questions unasked. They proceeded with the massage. I paid. I don't remember if I tipped them. It was probably "cash only" for tips and I rarely carry cash, and usually only for parking emergencies.

Even though this was about a decade ago, my friend and I laugh about it to this day. We're still friends if you can believe that.

This experience has turned me into a foot massage connoisseur. I just try to find the places that don't take smoke breaks between tissue tenderizing. I even had a punch card at my favorite spot about ten years ago. I was training for half marathons, and after a long run, I would treat myself to a foot soak and massage. Every tenth massage was free, so I would take friends and offer to pay for them so I could get more punches faster. This isn't really a story of how I saved money, I just want you to know that I can commit to SOMETHING—for the right price and the right punch card.

My most recent foot spa adventure landed me at a cozy little chain in Santa Barbara, California. During COVID-19, massage establishments could only operate outside as a way of reopening for business. I had not had a massage in about eight months. I count the time between massages like some people might count time between relationships. Each massage gives me back precious drops of my life force. I had become quite accustomed to this practice of paying someone to touch me in the name of health and well-being.

Prior to the pandemic, my masseuse became one of my best friends. We would do my astrology chart and speak in Spanish during the massage. She gave me life advice. I cried sometimes. In part, I cried due to the pain of my tense muscles and in part due to the pain of my tense life. Her hands brought me back to life at a point in my own sojourn where I didn't know if I could continue on continuing on. I love her. She retired during the pandemic, so I'll never get another massage from her again. The loss of this is nearly unrecoverable. But it didn't prevent me from staying in the game.

In Santa Barbara, the rainbow-esque sign above the door read "Outdoor Massage" in big, bold, capitalized yellow letters. Much like Master Wong's, the sign beckoned me. I was a moth to the flame. My deprived, untouched skin was only too desperate to transact money to make strangers touch me. (I'm just saying, if you think about it, it's a bit weird, right?) I asked for a ninety-minute, full-body massage with the foot soak.

The great thing about the confinement-period-turned-semi-open-period is that there was a preciousness to the fact that you might never be able to do this thing again. The world might shut down...again. You might die. You might be afraid and stay inside. The business might go out of business. Permanently. Everyone you love might retire. You might run out of income. You might run out of jokes. Everyone you love might decide never to leave their house again. You might never hug another human. Master Wong's spa is no longer in operation, but this has zero correlation to the pandemic. The only rational way to deal with the precipitous fragility of any experience that might be taken away is to live it to the maximum. So, I was out $55 for a ninety-minute massage in case you're a math person and care about the numbers. I graduated up.

I was led to an outdoor massage table. There were screens between me and the cars, but I could smell the heat and fuel exhaust off the warm parking lot asphalt. I could hear the footsteps of people exiting and entering the tea shop next door. I could smell the gasoline pump run off from the Arco gas station across the way. Skateboarding kids came by and couldn't bust their tricks because there was a lot of crashing and gnashing sounds. And the fire station directly across from me in the parking lot was in full operation and launched multiple sirens during my 1.5 hours of bliss. No matter.

Masked up, I was dizzy from my own lack of free and clear breathing. My feet were in boiling water. It was over ninety degrees outside. Every single muscle on my body hurt. But I was honed, experienced, even worldly now. I knew what was coming. The pulverizing began.

About halfway through, after the latest siren departure, I was told to take off all my clothes. *Excuse me?* I was half asleep and deoxygenated from my face mask. "What?" I understood him perfectly well but was acting dumb because, well, I wanted to see what would happen next.

Here's the thing. I like to think I'm smarter than I am. I worry I overthink and I worry I under-think and I usually err on the side of semi-over-preparation. Some people who love me tell me I think too much. What is enough thinking, to be exact?

Because I thought I was being smart, I decided to prepare for my outdoor table massage by wearing a dress with a built-in bra. This would maximize the clothed massage by minimizing the layers between me, the towel and the stranger trying to fix my back that creaked and cricked more than a decrepit wooden house in a hurricane. I mean, it was audibly cracking. If my back was a candy, it would have been PopRocks.

I'm not often worried about what is lost in translation. I figure what I don't know right now can't hurt me. But I was told to take off my clothes. Remember, there was no barrier between me and the other patrons. So, you know what I did? I crawled under the towel and took off the top part of my dress, because pain wins out over decency. I've learned in my decision-making matrix of what to do under unusual circumstances is accept being temporarily, publicly clothesless if there's a possibility of alleviating my pain.

This is what the pandemic did to me: it made me a more-often semi-public nudist more than usual, all in the name of momentarily erasing my touch deprivation tank and easing me into a state of semi-relaxation. (Note to my parents who are reading this: I was still mostly covered with a towel and stuff. And no one could see me, anyway, because we were all wearing masks up and over our nosebridges and washcloths over our eyeballs.)

I woke up the next day. I could barely move. I was so, so sore. Tender to my own touch, my muscles ached, and I felt I must have looked black and blue. I could barely play tennis the next day, which I assured my coach was not because I was still doing prison workouts. I stopped those because they threw a wrench in my wrist earlier that year. "I can't move because I got a parking lot, deep-tissue massage," I told him. I often encounter people in my life who respond to me with a knowing nod as if to say, "No further questions."

Thai Massage

When I was in graduate school studying business administration, my soul was crushed more than it was exalted. The program might have been more aptly called, "How to Be a Middle Manager in Corporate America whilst Pushing Papers, People, and Products to an Agonizing Finish Line on a Moving Target Where No One Remembers Why We're Even Doing What We're Doing in the First Place." But they called it an MBA to make it short, tidy, and marketable.

My weekday schedule went something like this: wake up at 5:00 a.m., commute to work by 6:00 a.m., work from 6:00 a.m.-3:00 p.m., commute to school from 3:00 p.m.-4:00 p.m., do homework from 4:00 p.m.-6:00 p.m., go to class and seem awake and engaged from 6:00 p.m.-10:00 p.m. Afterward, I would reward myself with Wendy's $0.99 spicy chicken nuggets and listen to Dr. Drew Pinsky dissect intimate details of other people's relationship issues on Loveline. On a particularly special evening, I would add a $0.99 Frosty and $0.99 French fry order for a trifecta of pleasure. I would proceed to bed with a full stomach by 11:30 p.m. Wake up. Restart. Apparently, I existed in this ludicrous liminal space long enough to get a degree and not get fired. At least there's a piece of paper in a drawer somewhere that says I graduated, and I'm willing to believe it at this point.

On the days I was not in a physical building for class, due to this newfangled idea of online schooling or simply having an "off" night to do homework and research, I had a plan. The plan was simple: never do a grad school assignment without a glass of beer or wine in hand. I figured that if a former English Literature major, nose-in-a-book, mamby-pamby Humanities softie like me could soldier through business school (b-school, as it's called), then I should do it Hemingway-style. Non-sober. Likely, this explains my first ever C- in Advanced Financial Analysis. If you ever need someone to calculate your weighted average cost of capital for mergers and acquisitions, please, for the love of all things decent and lovely and mildly good in this world, do not call me. Do not email me. Do not even think of me.

The difference between me in graduate school and

undergraduate school was simple: perfectly sober (undergrad) versus happily un-sober (graduate school). I could tell you, to this day, exactly which classes I received a B in during undergrad. There were only four Bs in four years. To this day, it's hard for me to remember my Social Security Number, but I remember exactly why I didn't get an A in each class. In one instance, I proudly argued my way up from a C to a B. I should have received a C because while I attended every class (I think), I slept in the back row with my hoodie on. In my defense, it was a class on the history of grammar, which would literally bore anyone to death. The fact that I merely slept and didn't actually succumb to death was a feat in and of itself. Apparently, this whole business of sleeping in class was disrespectful to both the professor and my aptitude, he told me. He also told me if I didn't start thinking critically that I would flush all my potential down the toilet. Maybe he's partly to blame and partly to thank for my worrying habits.

Graduate school was a much different beast, and so was I by that time. I learned quickly I could score points by debating. This very skill—debate—in undergrad had me thrown out of my freshman writing course. See, I made my opponent cry. I won, for the record, in case you're keeping score. But I won through forcefulness and fervor. "No other freshman college students are interested in intellectual debates at 8:00 a.m.," my professor informed me. She was the same professor who asked me to debate.

After making that young lady cry at 8:00 a.m. during Writing 101, the only thing that the school officials could think to do with me was throw me into an honor's class with other "smart people." Oh, and suggest, officially, that I transfer schools. I stayed. What do they know?

In graduate school I gained material, extra points for debating. It was a part of my grade. They typecast me and assigned me a debate perspective they thought would be the opposite of my own viewpoint. The thing my professors never grasped is that I like to debate just to debate; just to hear myself talk. And make other people cry, if I'm lucky. One professor told me I should drop out and go to law school. What do they know? It's happened to me quite a lot, people telling me to drop out and stuff and become someone else. I plod along. No one understands this undue burden of my life like I do.

Graduate school was really a marathon. The work was not too intellectually taxing, although I went to a highly accredited school with letters they assured me would really matter on a resume. Let me debunk this: the acronyms of a university have never mattered in the working world. No one has ever given a flying rip about my MBA. Or the fancy "AACSB" accreditation tacked on. Yet, I list it out on my resume. Every time. Because I paid for it.

Due to my consumption of junk food, vicarious nightly radiotherapy instead of fixing my own life, and lack of sleep, my morning commute at 5:15 a.m. was pretty tenuous. I fell asleep at the wheel for a split second a couple times, which is virtually the road episode of *Scared Straight*. I was scared, all right.

One morning, indistinct from all others in the perpetual hamster wheel of self-inflicted pain without gain, I was rear-ended. I took stock. First, I celebrated it wasn't my fault. I had not fallen asleep at the wheel of a car—just the wheel of my life. I was not bodily injured, that I knew of. My car was "totaled," according to the insurance claim which paid me the full Kelley Blue Book Value of my vehicle. The car, who was affectionately known as Grandma, had been legally totaled. My first vehicle. I never got the body work done; I figured pocketing the cash made more sense. I needed to fund my spicy chicken nugget habit and pay for a trip to Hawaii.

After finishing up the initial police reporting post-accident, I took the day off from work, and went to urgent care. Urgent care check-ups are another relatively useless, bureaucratically induced process of paying money to find out you're not dead. I mean, sometimes it helps to have someone tell me out loud that I'm still alive. When I was in that period of my life, I felt dead on a normal, daily basis. So for them to give me medical clearance to keep living was probably worth my $20 copay.

After receiving notification, officially, that I was alive and somewhat well, I decided to undertake what was, in hindsight, a very suspicious decision: I got my first Thai massage the day of this car accident. What is a life if not to be lived? And what of a life that feels downtrodden, if not to pay someone to step on you?

I was in the middle of Claremont Village, which is an idyllic, small town, Americana-feeling place at the base of the Los Angeles National Forest. It was rated the fifth safest city in America, the streets were lined with trees, the houses had manicured lawns, and the bakery sold out of my favorite cookies every Saturday. Yes, I consider cookies for breakfast an exemplary weekend option. Think about it. Inside, there are eggs, carbs, fruit. It is a full meal.

I stepped into a Thai Massage studio in a 1990s beige strip mall, adjacent to the railroad tracks. But when you're in the fifth safest city in America, being near the tracks is hip and cool with restaurants and stores lining the avenues. I entered and asked for the one-hour Thai Massage, paid, and was led into the locker room. At this time in my plucky, bright life, I was a solid XS size. I was handed a ladies XXL pair of shorts and an XXL T-shirt; I wasn't sure, exactly, how the shorts were going to stay up. "Put these on but take off your underwear," I was told. There are always a lot of rules to these things. I obliged.

I was led into a darkened room, wearing my more-than-a-few-sizes-too-big clothing, while I held up my pants. I was then instructed to lie down on the floor mat, belly down. I peeked up momentarily to see poles on the ceiling with curtains and scarves hanging down. "Take a deep breath," she said. And she stepped on me.

I wasn't aware that I was paying to get stomped on. It was a new sensation, to be sure. My back has always had a slightly geriatric flavor to it with spinal fusion, vertebrae compression, and muscles taut like sailing ropes. "Stress," my doctor says. *Worry dedication*, I say internally. As she stepped on my back, loosening my muscles and cracking my spine to what sounded like the "pop" part of popcorn, she held the scarves on the roof for support.

Where things got really interesting is when she went down on hands and knees to knead out my shoulders like bread dough. It was rough and vigorous and I wasn't sure if she'd break me before my knots broke her hands. Literally, we were in an energetic tug-of-war. I couldn't breathe by the time her knee shoved into my latissimus dorsi muscle. Perhaps because my lungs were on the other side of that, smashed into a 1" floor cushion, I started coughing convulsively and wondered if this was how I would meet my end.

"Take off your shirt." Here we go again. I shimmied and shifted and complied. "Do you want lotion or no lotion?" I puzzled. "What's the difference?" I asked. "Lotion is American, no lotion is Thai." It might have been a matter of ego, wanting to fit in somehow and look "natural," or trying to appear like I'm the kind of person who "goes with the flow," but for whatever reason, I said no lotion.

What proceeded next was worse than the knee-to-lat-lung-puncture series of exasperation. She rubbed my back muscles, strenuously, with no lotion. No oil. No love. It felt like sandpaper on my trodden skin. Mere hours prior, I was grateful I hadn't fallen asleep and caused the car accident. Then I wondered how I ended up paying to be tortured at the subdermal layer of my existence.

I think a few tears eked out. I wasn't sure if the response should have been, "Please stop torturing me," or "I hate all of my life choices." I have no idea how to ask for the things I need. "I need therapy? I just got in a car accident today, and this is way worse?"

By the time she got to my calves and feet, I felt raw. Maybe I astral projected away from my earthly body to avoid the rest of the sensation of this experience, because I can't really tell you how it ended. I don't remember leaving or what I ate that day. Or even how I felt the next day.

And if you're curious—yes, I've gotten a half-dozen or so Thai massages after that just to see if I really like the experience or not. The jury is still out. Testing has been temporarily suspended. In the name of scientific research and expansion of ideas, I didn't want to rule out an entire massage option just because I had the bright idea to get my back smashed the day I got my car smashed.

My only takeaway is this: when asked if you want lotion or no lotion, just take the damn lotion.

Korean Spa

The only thing I knew about Korean spas before I entered my first time was that you have to get naked. It's gender-segregated and there's no funny business. But you are not allowed to wear bathing wear into the hot tubs or saunas. Further, you cannot shower in private. There are no walls on the shower stalls. In fact, there are mirrors. You can watch yourself shower naked, while watching your neighbor. Finally, you are massaged, bare naked, in front of other exposed humans. Your masseur will, however, be wearing a bra and panties.

I was not all that nervous about the naked part. But when I checked in, I was handed a watch that served as my billing device and my locker key, a T-shirt, and paper slippers. "Take off your shoes when you're downstairs," they said. I did. I grabbed a pair of pleated shorts. These were to be worn in the communal area, called the Jimjilbang.

I went to my locker, unlocked it with my wristwatch, and stripped naked. I put a towel over me, but of course, everyone was about to see everything, anyway. I wandered into the wet room. My chief concern was not to look like I didn't know what I was doing. But in general, it's hard to look around at others to get information about what I should be doing without seeming like a creep. So, I adopted a posture of moving slowly and keeping my eyes mostly lowered.

First stop: you grab a disposable toothbrush and toothpaste. Put it, dry, in your mouth. Go to the stand-up shower, which is open-air, breezily next to the other people in the stand-up showers. Brush your teeth heartily while lathering generously. Since I was homeschooled, I never experienced locker rooms, but I suppose this isn't shocking to athletes. For me, it was my first time being around a herd of unknown naked people.

I slipped into the warm tub. It was deliciously freeing, warmer than a normal bath at home. I soaked it all in. I meandered across the wall to the hot tub. As I initially turned pinker than a shrimp glimmering in the sunshine, there was no mistaking the difference between a "warm" tub and this "hot" tub. My skin instantly turned a deeper, darker lobster red. I broiled myself just a little longer than what feels natural.

As I lifted my eyes, perilously peeking to take in my soundings, I saw all shapes and sizes of women. So much diversity in color and culture. And all ages. Korean moms had toddlers on their hips while they escorted their grandmas into the tub. Four generations of naked women bathed together in the warm tub, while children mostly didn't enter the hot tub. It was seriously steaming.

While others might claim they enjoy people watching whilst out and about, I much prefer auditory allowance...also known as eavesdropping. I like to think of it as dialectic research for future writings. The way some people have photographic memories, I seem to have auditory imprints that never go away. Haunting conversations replay over and over—ones I'd rather forget, sometimes. The thing I overheard the most, spoken by women who looked a bit like me at the time—twenty-something, white-ish to start and advancing to lobster-red in the hot tub—is, "What a relief it is to see so many different types of people." It was a dawning of relief to remember we're all fleshy, gooey cells replicating rapidly while we're all different, beautiful, and unique. Sturdy, strong, and soft all at the same time. Women are wondrous, aren't we?

After my skin-seafood bake in the hot tub, I proceeded to a cold plunge. The cold tub was short, deep, and entered by a ladder. The goal is full-body submersion. If you're brave and bold, you'll bounce between the hot tub and cold plunge several times. Apparently, this is good for anti-inflammation and blood circulation. It definitely helps me feel alive, at bare minimum. Placing my shoulders underneath the icy water (which was about fifty-eight degrees), I bounced up and down just to know if my limbs still worked.

Next, it was time to steam myself. At that point, I was more like cobbed corn, going to get slick, puffy, and bubbly if I was lucky. The wet steam room was 120 degrees, filled with granite tiles. The steam was palatable, it penetrated my body and swirled around as I sat down on the tile. It burned my nakedness in places that never saw the light of day. Ducking out briefly, I grabbed a towel outside and went for round two. My lips, in particular, were stinging. I folded them inside of themselves, literally gritting and bearing it.

I slowed my breathing. The only way to survive in that type of thing is to become one with the experience, surrendering to the fact that you're roasting alive and paying to do so. No one else in the room seemed phased by the heat. I think, perhaps, I was weak from hunger, as I simultaneously lost my appetite to the oppressive humidity. (Even if there is an earthquake, my first question is usually, "Am I experiencing this dizziness due to hunger or is this an actual natural disaster in progress?" I attribute hunger to many things gone awry. Maybe that's why I accidentally got married. Divorce reason? I was hangry.) I stayed in the steam room as long as I could, making each inhale match the length of the exhale. When I saw women who must be in their eighties taking such an experience head-on without apparent distress, I wondered if this slow, deep breathing while under heat pressure might be the secret to anti-aging. In fact, everyone seemed to like it.

I exited the humid steam room, panting and reaching for air unlaced with moist heat. A lady waved at me to come under a showerhead. With exuberance, she pulled the lever. A rush of freezing cold ice water descended on me from a rainfall shower head. It was simultaneously obstructive, horrid, invigorating. And she laughed. A full of gusto, nothing held back kind of belly laugh. I bowed slightly and said the only word in Korean I know, "Annyeonghaseyo (안녕하세요)," which garnered me more glee. She pulled the lever again.

Looking like a wet dog, hair matted to my face in all directions, and skin prickly to the touch as my hair stood up on end like cactus spines, I wandered into the dry sauna. This room was a balmy 160-180 degrees. On the television inside the sauna, which seemed normal to everyone else but me, there were Korean soap operas and game shows playing. Women fanned themselves lazily. I put my towel down on the bench and dried off in mere seconds from my cold waterfall experience. Women gossiped in Korean. Some women fell fast asleep. I remained. I watched the clock outside until it had been five minutes, which seemed like all I could bear. (Future spoiler: I can do a solid twenty to thirty minutes now. I've trained.)

If life is a delicate balance between north and south magnets, fire and water, male and female energies, and cold and hot, then

I think I took in way too much heat that day. It was time to call it. And by "call it," I mean I needed to take a lukewarm shower to get all the steam sweat off.

I spied the sit-down showers. Mostly, they were used by elderly Korean women. There are parts to the ritual I still don't fully understand. I made my way to a stall by the wall...a way of feeling semi-private in my fully exposed state.

I crouched onto the stool. I am a short person, so this was not difficult. The shower wand came away from the wall, and I adjusted it to a tepid warmth. I was sitting, fully naked, in front of a personal mirror. Showering while sitting down in front of a mirror was a new experience. So there I was, staring at myself whilst showering. I started to cry, softly. Not because I was thinking of the song "[Wo]Man in the Mirror" by Michael Jackson and reviewing all of my life choices and character fables and flaws. But because I'd never seen myself like that.

I mean, *really* seen myself. I didn't know I had that wrinkle or that flab or that elasticity. There was a lot of judgment. There was a lot of shame. There was some gratitude. And a little triumph. Like, "I'm me. I made it this far. This is who I am." Seeing myself, fully, for the first time. I hated it. I cried until the mirror steamed. I wished no one was looking, but I was grateful to be naked in public and so un-seen at the same time.

Our society is full of dichotomous moments like this—being completely naked amongst strangers who don't see you. Seeing yourself, clearly, for the first time amongst a crowded room. Realizing all we have is this very present moment, the cells stitch together our experiences of this tangible, mutable, physical, and yet metaphysical world and wondering what it all means, if there is any meaning to be found at all. Existentialism. The being and becoming-ness of it all struck me as I showered.

I washed. And I wondered. And I wondered while I washed.

I popped back into the chlorinated warm tub after shower number two. I thought, *I'm done with the heat, for now.* And I awaited my massage. My number was called up—the same number on my wristband watch used as my wallet and locker key. So efficient! It was time to go.

I walked into the room next door, with rows of massage tables covered in plastic so they could be easily washed down between customers. I slid onto one as directed, trying to catch myself as I almost slipped off. It was as slick as a Slip 'N Slide with me being about as shrively and wet as a drowned rat. The first step began. With a yellow mit in hand that looked like something to wash cars, I was lathered in soap and my skin proceeded to receive a scrub. Similar to sandpaper, my masseur took the first layer of skin off. I'll spare you the full details, but trust me when I say you can visibly see yourself molting layers of your own skin. My reptilian brain remembered the lizard phase of my evolution when I saw skin slicing off with each spirited scrub.

Every—now, I truly mean *every*—inch of you is scrubbed. Mercilessly. I was flipped over onto each side, onto my stomach, onto my back. With each movement I tried not to skim off the slick surface of the table. I whimpered. It hurt like heck. Especially under my armpits. Other places, too. I had to remind myself I wanted the authentic, full experience.

I was showered off the table. "Here, go wash your face." I was allowed to wash my own face. And I was told to sit in the dry sauna to dry off. I went back to the open showers, scrubbed my face rapidly, and popped back into the 160-degree furnace until I was dry and toasty again.

Back for more abuse. I found my table, less wet and wild at that point, and laid down. There was a foil blanket draping the table. I was rubbed down in paraffin wax (like the kind you get for a manicure or pedicure, but over the entirety of my body). Then, I lit up like a candle. Upon the final application of wax, the edges of the foil blanket tucked me in. I began to heat the wax with my body temperature and emergency blanket, thinking, *This is what it must feel like to be a baked fish.*

Another shower on the massage table followed. She washed my hair and conditioned it before wrapping it tighter than a steel drum into a toweled top knot. I thought of how little my own grandmas touched me. They never played with my hair or braided it. I only remember hugs. It was strange to be this intimate with a stranger.

After about forty minutes in, the main event and massage itself began. I was drenched in oil. It felt like the salad course following the baked white, flaky fish course. I was oiled up and then rubbed as unsparingly as I was scrubbed down. The strokes were similar and the vigor was just as vital. Similar to the scrub, I was massaged everywhere.

I'm not sure if it felt good. It was just...full of feels. Sometimes that's enough.

After being slapped on the back and told, "Time's up," I was handed a white robe and my hand was stuffed with an empty tip envelope. I gingerly waddled out of the wet room so as not to slip and placed a $20 bill into the envelope. I learned how to say thank you (감사합니다) many years later. Instead, I just repeated: *annyeonghaseyo* (안녕하세요) to say goodbye. I meant it. *Thank you*, I said in my heart. *I feel changed, somehow.*

Following my fruitful foray into Korean massage, there was still more to discover at the spa. I donned the apparel of an elementary school gym class: a goldenrod yellow T-shirt and pleated beige shorts a couple of sizes too big. Five flights of stairs up, I alighted in the Jimjilbang. This was the family friendly, mixed gender space where couples and families congregated to eat, nap, read, watch television, use a computer, check out a book from the library, and play.

I walked into the cafe and ordered one of my favorite Korean meals: a bulgogi bento box. Of course, the bento box is Japanese. But this is Los Angeles we're talking about, and cultures borrow avidly from one another. I inhaled my miso soup (also Japanese), kimchi (the best fermented food on the planet), and sticky rice with sautéed, sugary-salty beef. It was heavenly. I also ordered a skin-cleansing juice of kale and pineapple. *Life*, I thought, *could not be better.* Food resolves most existential questions, longings, and heartaches. A full belly is a more fun philosophy.

The next round of heatroom visiting approached. I headed into the salt room first. It was about 130 degrees, tiled in pink, and filled with pink Himalayan sea salt crystals lining the floor. FYI, they prick your feet if you don't wear your paper slippers. Sliding onto the salt, I grabbed a wooden pillow. Those are slatted pieces of wood meant to hold your neck while you lay down in the salt. I inhaled. I didn't smell anything but heat.

Next was the jade room. It wasn't as tactically stimulating as the salt room, but there were less people inside, which made it a tad more relaxing. The walls were lined with a mandala pattern of jade hues. Someone was doing yoga on a sleeping mat in the corner.

I made a quick stop into the 200-degree sauna, called the Bulgama. It cost over one million dollars to build this room. Spherical and hut-like, it was heated to a level that I am not sure how humans can stand for the recommended ten to fifteen minutes. I took a towel in to stand upon, as my feet could not take the heat. My lips threatened to melt off. My eyelids were singed immediately upon entrance. I saw older Korean folks who'd been there before I entered, and presumably outlasted me, as they didn't look like they were going anywhere in a hurry. Their heads were bent in prayer or meditation. I wondered what it would be like to withstand this suffering in silence and stillness. I didn't wait to find out.

I took a breath outside. I laid down on a sleeping mat. It was a 1" padded mat, placed on a heated tile floor. I let my back expand from the cozy comfort of the floor, splaying my feet out. I relaxed, but there were more saunas to conquer.

The final foray was into the clay pit. Imported from Korea, the room was filled with small clay balls. Imagine a ball pit, but with bead-sized clay. It was deep and hard to walk in without falling over. This is supposedly the most medicinal of all experiences as it is supposed to stimulate the lymphatic system and detoxify heavy metals from your body. Korean soap operas played lazily in the background. The weather news came on at some point. I sunk deeper, shimmying my body down into the layers of clay. I put some of the clay on top of my stomach, my chest, and overturned it in my hands. It's a kinesthetic dream. I fell asleep like this.

After all the heat, and all the fish-like baking, I tackled the cold room. This was the last step before shower number 267. Icicles covered the walls and melted precipitously as it was only forty-six degrees inside. I saddled up to the tiled wall and allowed the heat to escape from my back. Sitting cross-legged, I invited the cold to enter all my joints and bring me back down to earth.

My clothes smelled like the earth. My calves were stained with clay. I had salt stuck in my pockets. And I thought, *I have been somewhere. A journey of a few steps into a new world.*

I motioned myself down the stairs, back to the women's area. I showered, again. I brushed my teeth, again. I washed and conditioned my hair, again.

I grabbed a new pair of clothes and a fresh robe. I made my way into the sleeping room. With a couple of blankets I found, I crafted a tiny nest in the darkened corner. The pillow was a cushioned block. I nestled in. And in a room full of unfamiliar women, in a strange place, I felt quite at home. And I slept.

After Christmas gatherings, I would come here to molt.

After my birthday, I would shed my literal, old skin.

After my divorce, I came here to cry.

The day I left my marriage in order to start my new life, I came and got a massage. Every cell in my body was crying. The level of excruciating emotional pain was unmatched. Tears welled in my eyes during the scrub, and the lady started singing to me softly in Korean. When she washed my hair, I hummed the lyrics of "I'm Going to Wash that Man Out of My Hair" from South Pacific. It was the only Korean massage I've ever had that was tender to the touch; tender enough to match my tender heart and head full of broken dreams.

I only go to one Korean spa. When you know, you know. You find the one and you don't leave. I can be loyal, sometimes.

Upon entrance, each time I arrive, I proudly announce, "I love this place the way some people like theme parks," which usually gets me a slight smile and never a gusty laugh from the folks at the front desk. But I mean it with all my heart. I found my place.

I worry I'll never go back.

As this chapter was written, my favorite-ever spa in Koreatown, Los Angeles closed for over six months due to the global pandemic of COVID-19. For just a brief moment, I thought about going there for "research." Then, I remembered it was closed. Who knows when it will reopen? Who knows *if* it will reopen?

I worry I'll never feel as blistered and beautiful as I do on a day at the Korean spa. I worry the place that taught me to see myself, in all my fabulousness and with all my flaws, will not survive. It felt like a part of me was dying as I wrote this.

As kids, we would make forts to escape life and pretend we were elsewhere. This was the Korean spa for me. It was my hideaway, my home away from home. And when I had no home, it was truly my literal and actual home (if but for a few days).

I've never lived anywhere more than two years continuously as an adult. I've lived in seventeen places since age seventeen. In 2020, I moved four times. Like many people, I've rebuilt my whole life during the pandemic after saying goodbye to my job, my career, my love of chicken and waffles, my home, my relationship, my ego, and even my body (I traded it in for a new one).

I long for one constant. The Korean spa was my constant. And it, too, is gone. Temporal. Fleeting.

Being in motion suits me, though. I am a bit of a nomadic soul. But even nomads need a pit stop. And the Korean spa is my favorite, forever stop. My heart metaphorically manifested itself into this building—a building filled with boiling water, and sandpaper scrubs, and saunas hotter than Hades itself. I know, because I've been to hell and back just a couple of times. (It's called divorce, y'all.)

This is what I know: if I can survive a 200-degree furnace, I can survive anything life will throw at me. Bring it.

Chapter 9

Let's Worry about Breakups

The thing feminism stole from my generation is the ability to choose to be a housewife. By the mid-2000s, in upper echelon coastal elite cities, this was no longer seen as a legitimate, celebrated, distinguished career. Gone are the days where you can create value from cooking, cleaning, and child-rearing. Now it's all about getting a fancy degree no one ever asks you about and climbing a corporate ladder that more closely resembles the Leaning Tower of Pisa. You're allegedly going up, but the path is so wonky and off-center it's hard to tell if you're making progress or merely falling forward. And usually, it's a combination therein.

I'd liked to have had the option to apply to be a wife and homemaker. Is this a bygone tradition? Other than inserting an advertisement for myself in a mail-order bride catalog, which reeks of general unbecomingness, I'm not sure where one applies. "Hello, I'd like to be gainfully employed as your life partner and paid (non-monetarily) to sit at home and manage things." "What things?" "Things that come up. Things that don't come up. Isn't it better if you don't even know what goes into running a household and simply allow me to take care of it?" I always thought the best situational management is the kind you don't even know exists. Naturally, this makes value attribution difficult, but there's bound to be another department for that. I'd lay out a meal of pan con tomate, pappardelle with artichokes and asparagus topped with crispy prosciutto, and open a perfectly paired Barolo wine. Housewife, chef, and sommelier goals for the win. Who says you can't go for the gold?

Some of the people in my life tell me that I would be bored as a housewife. "You could never stay at home and do nothing," they say. Obviously, to prove the naysayers wrong, I live my life like a *Seinfeld* episode. There are lots of people coming and going, the scenes are standalone while being hilarious, nothing really happens, and the plot doesn't advance. I also took up tennis and horseback riding to prove I could in fact be happy whilst doing nothing. And I absolutely, unequivocally love my life.

If I could go back in time and choose a mentor, it would be Carole Middleton. She had the enterprising vision to help her daughter, Kate, become a duchess. Yes, Kate works. Yes, she's a housewife. Yes, she's a part of the world's richest family. Her sister married a billionaire. This is the best of all possible worlds. With 20/20 hindsight, I see that perhaps a path that more closely mirrored the Middleton sisters could have yielded me a certain brand of happiness. If you cannot be born an heiress, become one.

Alas, I can't rewind my choices. I can simply review them.

No one sets out upon their life course to become an expert in breaking up. So, to save you heartache and hours of deliberation over your past, I'll help you worry about everything up front.

I've organized what to worry about when breaking up around a timeline or a unique type of situation. This will help you determine exactly what to worry about when. If you can match worry to when and how, then you're on to something really brilliant. Because now you can have the satisfaction of knowing you're just on time to ruin your life. Or fix it, depending on if you're a glass half-full or a glass half-empty person. I'm usually a fill it up person, if we're speaking about some alcohol in a glass. If the glass isn't at capacity, rectify immediately. I think this should end all discussions about glasses being in any capacity of spaciousness. Simplify things, and top it off.

Timelines and Types of Breakups and What to Worry About

Breaking Up Too Soon

Once upon a time, I was being driven around in a beat-up Nissan Sentra, running errands, with a friend who I had only known a month or so.

Some races are over before they've even begun. I was seventeen, it was my first year in college. I didn't own a car, so my leading way of making friends was to see who *did* own a car. That way, I could make friends with them while they drove me around town.

My standards were fairly low. It wasn't even a nice car. It was a low-key afternoon, we were just driving around, doing whatever errands college students do (also, what did I need to run errands for? My books—the only thing I needed—were already at my dorm). I was mostly minding my own business, and while at a stoplight he asked, "Do you think we should get married?"

I hesitated, and checked to see if the doors were locked or if I could make a getaway on foot. Then, I had to weigh out the danger of running around the urban streets of Los Angeles without knowing where I was versus riding in the car with him after I had to break the news to him that no, I didn't think we should get married.

This was one of the seven times I was proposed to by the age of eighteen.

Breaking Up Too Late

Once upon a time, I was barely a legal-aged adult, nearly a child bride. At my first wedding, I was twenty years old. I had just turned twenty the month before, so I would say I was a young twenty.

My Matron of Honor was in line to proceed into the church to have the ceremony to legally bind me to another human being. As we were waiting in the hallway, she turned to me and asked, "Do you want to run away? Now is your last chance."

I had my arm laced in my dad's as he was preparing to walk me down the aisle. I wanted both my parents to walk me down the aisle as I am less traditional than some people I know. I'm not sure he heard her. I was annoyed at the question. But looking back, I'm annoyed at the version of me who didn't run because the sunk cost of a wedding is less of an economic burn than having your whole life go up in flames, liquidating assets, selling a house, and leaving with $40 in your pocket and merely the clothes on your back six years later.

In hindsight, I broke up too late. I should've run before arriving at the altar. And if nothing else, this whole business was bad for the profit and loss ledger of my life. So, save yourself money, watch the warning signs, and break up before it's too late to save yourself money. Your future P&L might thank you.

Breaking Up before It Gets Interesting

Once upon a time, I broke up with someone who wanted to live the rest of his life in Russia. He wanted to move there, and never return to America.

I like wearing flip-flops. Unrelated, I also decided not to go to one particular private college in Southern California because they banned flip-flops in class. I take marriage and collegiate decisions seriously when it comes to appropriate footwear. And the less footwear, the better. If you have to have footwear in life, at least wear sandals. And the least sandal-y sandals, the better. The less straps and do-dads and crossovers and ties, the happier I am. So, I broke up with him because I didn't want to move to Russia indefinitely. It sounded cold. And I am a warm kind of person.

Alas, it is possible I broke up before things got interesting. I might have enjoyed learning about the Kremlin. I might have enjoyed Siberian temperatures. I might have enjoyed being an expatriate in a country that hates my countryman. I might have met Julian Assange. I might have eaten caviar for breakfast every day. I might have become funnier than I am now because I would have had nothing else to do but make up jokes. I also might have ended up in prison for making jokes because there are less freedoms of speeches and the like.

The thing is, sometimes you cut things off early and you miss stuff. But, I still have flip-flops, and they've done me right all these years.

Breaking Up over the Telephone

Once upon a time, a very nice, very handsome, very athletic-looking tennis coach called me up one day to ask me out on a date. He telephoned me. Working at a five-star resort, I was a hostess at the beachside restaurant while he worked at the hotel's tennis courts. The date request was perfectly nice and perfectly reasonable: a bonfire with his sister and a group of their high school friends.

"You don't even know who I am," I said, and I slammed the receiver down. I am a slippery eel to catch. He had the audacity to call again, and explain he *did*, in fact, know who I was—and would *still* like to ask me out on a date, despite the fact that I hung up on him.

My cheeks turned ruby red, and I stammered. I'm not usually lost for words, as you can tell from this winding manuscript. I don't remember what I said or why I didn't want to go out with him (he was very cute and apparently *did* know who I was...).

So the best way to end a relationship over the telephone, in summary, is to hang up the first time and don't take the second call. I'm sorry, young fellow.

I don't even remember his name. Turns out *I* was the one who didn't really know who *he* was, and I never saw him again.

Breaking Up by Proxy

Once upon a time, I went on a charity date. The scenario goes something like this: I liked a boy who had a roommate. The roommate liked me. The boy I liked wanted to get rid of me, so he told me that his roommate had a crush on me. "Okay," I said. "But I don't have a crush on him." The boy I liked proceeded to tell me that I had to date his roommate because his roommate had low self-esteem. I was informed, and mildly threatened, that if I didn't go out with him, then his friend would never go out with another human being again.

I like to think of myself as generally helpful. So I went on a pity date with the roommate, but said it was casual. "Don't expect a second date," I told them both. I think we went on the second date for good measure, just to build up his self-esteem before I said the inevitable goodbye. But he didn't pay for my coffee, which was a super bummer. Being that I was a college student, and with my limited charity dating experience, I was not expecting to have to donate myself a coffee, and I couldn't even write it off during tax season.

I told the boy I liked that I no longer wanted to go out with his roommate and informed him that it was his job to break us up since he wrangled me into this charity dating scheme to begin with. Both boys were upset at me, depressed, and I made at least one—but probably both—of them cry.

I vowed no more charity dates. And, when needing to break up with someone by proxy, make sure you engage a neutral, third-party service. Preferably, elect someone who won't cry whilst doing your dirty work.

Breaking Up after IHOP

Once upon a time, a man I wasn't sure I wanted to date asked me out. I suggested we could go on a breakfast date. I figured the likelihood of unsafe and unsavory behavior over pancakes was limited.

My mom warned me of date rape drugs when I went to college, so I figured I could see easily if someone was trying to slip something into my grapefruit juice or coffee. He offered to pick me up. I said I'd meet him there. He was actually very sweet and brought me flowers (a first). But I didn't go on a second date because he wanted to take me out dancing. I wasn't twenty-one yet, and didn't want to do anything illegal like sneak into a club.

The thing is, if you can only go on one date before you break up, IHOP is a pretty good choice. It's safe. Harmless. There are families around. Nothing can go too far off the rails. And if you plan it right, you can order 2,000 calories in one meal, meaning you don't have to eat the rest of the day. If he pays, this is highly economical. I call this the "value date and ditch." I've been on two first and last dates to IHOP and the strategy remains strong.

Breaking Up on a Train

Once upon a time, I left on a train and never came home. I did not exactly break up on the train, but the train was my getaway vehicle. It's a brilliant way to put mileage between you and your soon-to-be-ex because you are not operating the heavy machinery alone. This gives you maximum time to cry without having to worry about weaving in and out of traffic and possibly crashing your car while you are simultaneously crashing your emotional life.

I quite recommend trains. I think trains are a highly underutilized form of transportation. They are roomy. They have trays. They have snacks and alcohol for sale. And they have WiFi.

I'm not sure why anyone travels by any other mode of transportation, really. Think about it. Trains are superior in so many ways. If you must plan a getaway to formulate your breakup plan, then I recommend a train.

Breaking Up over a Bowl of Mac and Cheese

Once upon a time, I made my ex-boyfriend a big bowl of mac and cheese. You might understand at this point, it is my favorite food. I am classy like that. I told him we should focus on being friends and give ourselves room for self-growth and self-exploration, as we were still young. He wanted to discuss marriage, but that felt heavier than carbs ladened in dairy. So to take the burden off, I suggested friendship and fun.

He didn't finish his bowl of mac and cheese, and told me we could never be just friends. I never saw him again. I cried and cried, and I ate his bowl of mac, and my own bowl of mac, and whatever was left in the pot, including licking the cheese sauce off of the spoon. Because, sometimes, the best way to engage in a breakup is to eat your feelings. Especially if they are salty and noodly and full of your favorite comfort food.

If you must break up while holding a bowl of your favorite food, you're in good shape. Unless you're the kind of person who can't eat after a breakup, in which case, this plan might be pure torture. You must decide for yourself.

And so, what do you do with the leftovers post-breakup, literally and metaphorically? If you have leftover mac and cheese, the only sensible thing is to eat the whole dang bowl, box, and whatever else you can find in the fridge to fortify yourself before you lose your appetite to the crying.

Without oversimplifying, here, it seems to me there are two kinds of people facing a breakup: those who hang on and those who purge. I'm the latter. And by *purge*, I mean I go all the way to erase the memory of said person ever having existed in a similar time-space reality to myself. I treat a breakup like the Watergate scandal data wipe: all evidence must go. Shred, fax, repeal, appeal, unseal, and trash it.

Here Is How I Put the "Break" into Breakups

Round One: The Generalized Purge

I delete all photographic evidence. I throw away jewelry. I toss out all the gifted items. I rip up clothing that was gifted. (I actually take scissors to it and shred it, just so you know.) I change my sheets, literally. All linens must be replaced: I get new sheets, new bed pillows, new throw pillows, new duvet covers, new dish towels, new washcloths, new placemats, new cloth napkins, new toilet paper. I buy new pajamas. Anything that anyone touched while touching me must go. I take down art that reminds me of the other person. I block them on social media, including LinkedIn so they cannot see my professional achievements (psyche, I became a writer so I have no professional achievements on LinkedIn anymore).

Round Two: Personhood Purge

I change all the parts of me that I had carved out while we were together. If I used to wear glasses, I get new glasses. (Just kidding, I gave up glasses altogether because I was a poser who wanted glasses and no longer needed them for prescription eye activities.) I change my hair. If I was a brunette when we were together, now I'm blonde. I never go red. I went red once and it was a very, very fire truck-looking tone of red and that was very, very bad. What if I didn't wear makeup while we were together because my ex hated me wearing makeup? Then, first stop, cosmetics shopping. I buy all the things at Sephora. I change my wardrobe. If we went on a date somewhere fancy? That dress, too, must pay the price and go. If I used to be fat when we were together? I'll lose weight. If I used to be skinny and sad when we were together? I'll get fat and happy. If there was an award for method acting whilst breaking up, I'd win. I'm an all-in, go-for-the-gold kind of a gal.

Round Three: Profusely Apologize Purge

I pretend I am in a twelve-step program. I apologize to everyone I ever knew. "I'm sorry I wasn't more me. I'm sorry I didn't tell the truth. I'm sorry I didn't ask for help. I'm sorry I missed the last five Christmases at your house, family." I've spent significant time sending emails to people I haven't talked to in five-plus years to make amends. It's like a cocktail: two parts awkward, one part heartwarming, with a twist that some people never reply.

Round Four: Polished Purge

I get a new career. If you break up and don't make up, it's a perfect time to reset all the pieces of your life. So, why not your job, too?

Some people think too much change at once is system shocking. I'm never sure how much change is enough change to not shock your system. But PastCass™ has figured if my system is already in shock, why not ride the wave into higher financial prosperity? If you're going to make wide, sweeping changes in your life, why not shoot for the moon and land amongst the stars with your income?

Round Five: Population Location Purge

I change my zip code. You most likely have to leave your dwelling, anyway. Why not change cities while you're at it?

I'm a real moving pro. I have it down to a couple hours flat, where I can pack up and call a stranger online to move my possessions into an undisclosed location and lock them into a storage unit. You can get a discount on your storage unit for first time sign-ups, so never plan to sign up with the same storage unit company.

Pro tip: everything in your life can be released in a few hours with this plan.

Round Six: Reconstruction

And now we've reached the arduous final climb wherein you have debated what to keep (nothing), dumped what is not serving (everything), and dedicated yourself to full recovery.

The difficult part is now reassembling the pieces of your life and making sense of what just happened. If all the sweeping changes you just made to create a new identity are worthy of a fresh start, where do you pick up that happy new life?

I wish Costco sold travel packages to "intern with the universe" or "become the better version of you." You can buy a thirty-one-country tour around Europe, but no one these days is selling a program where you just pick up and go and become the version of you that you want to be next. What would life be like if it were that easy to pay to simply become a new you? I suppose the commercials of this breakdown become an issue when you consider the factors of customer satisfaction and potential refund rates. "Can I get a refund on the new version of me I no longer like? What about upsells? If I want the base model of the new me with a couple of gilded items, what is that going to set me back? Can we commoditize self-growth?"

"I have no easy answers to these questions," says the gal who has engaged executive coaching, photography coaching, branding coaching, career coaching, digital media coaching, marketing coaching, publishing coaching, energy coaching, relationship coaching, and run-of-the-mill psychotherapy, too. I have paid a lot of money to become me and make sense of me in a world that doesn't always make sense.

The thing about breakups I didn't realize up front is that there are no refunds. There is no single relationship coach who can necessarily bring you through. You have to do the work yourself. And by work, I mean *feel*. To heal, you must feel.

I hate feeling so much I'd rather cry in protest than cry to feel my feelings. I would rather watch a video about hitting a pillow than actually punch the fabric. I would rather listen to someone cry on the phone and offer advice than shed a tear in front of another human.

But the only thing that seems to make any heap of difference is feeling the feelings all the way through. When I commit to actually doing this, it turns out, things get messy. I begin to treat my emotions like a science experiment. *What else could happen? What could come next? What could possibly go wrong?* I feel worried whenever anyone asks that question because there's probably more. *More what?* I don't know. Just more.

Ready for too much information? One time, while feeling my feelings all the way through, I got physically sick. I mean, I couldn't be away from the immediate vicinity of the restroom for over twenty-four hours. My body was so upset at holding emotions that I got the symptoms of the flu.

I also learned that I could cry so much that I would momentarily stop breathing. This seemed questionable. So, I tried to go just to the edge without dancing over the line.

I also learned I could cry until I threw up. This was particularly uncomfortable in many ways, from the convulsing and muscle tension and sweating and then you add vomiting to the mix.

I think heartbreak should be a medical condition. I would go into the doctor's office and explain the symptoms scientifically and with an air of composure: "Doctor, so good of you to see me on such short notice. I wasn't scheduled to have this existential midlife crisis until I was about fifty years old, but I'm an overachiever so I'm having it at thirty-one. Routinely, I have been experiencing irritable digestion and irregular appetites. I haven't eaten in days. I am watching my alcohol intake (literally, I watch it disappear out of my glass). I'm making sure to hydrate (by occasionally swapping water for wine, it's quite biblical the way I do it). However, I end up crying until I vomit. I'm having chest pains. I can't breathe some days. In clinical terms, I feel I am a hot mess." And the doctor would nod knowingly and poke my stomach and take my temperature and declare I shouldn't work or lift more than ten pounds for at least six months.

I could get sent to a health clinic, like an old-fashioned hotel in California where people used to recover from emphysema. I would play lawn games and lounge by the pool. And I would cry a lot. Maybe there would be groups. I would fill volumes and volumes of journals. And no one would expect anything from me except to fulfill the length of my stay with dignity. Then, at some later point, I could re-enter the world.

The thing is, breakups don't come with vacations. I'm not sure how anyone is supposed to manage a monumental recovery whilst crying until they can't eat, can't sleep, can't stand upright, and can't breathe. Yet, we don't have a diagnosis for this.

The only way to get over a breakup, it seems, is to finally find the day where you can laugh at yourself. Laugh at your choices. And have the courage to confront the past with the gift of grace. I say this nice stuff as a last resort, and only because I thought Mr. Clean Magic Erasers could bleach anything. But they weren't able to blot out the ink on the marriage certificates or divorce decrees, as it seems.

Maybe life itself is a cosmic joke. I'm still waiting for the punchline. When I asked the universe why it felt like my life was a joke, all I heard back was to tell jokes. So that's how I ended up here, in humor recovery. Healing with humor.

Chapter 10

Let's Worry about Losing Weight

Have you ever woken up on a seemingly ordinary day, only to find out your worst fears have been realized?

I can't tell you the exact moment of the day it happened or what I was wearing when I first heard the horrible news. I don't remember how it started...I think I just came to the realization quite the middle of it, kind of like being sucker-punched.

Bar none, my absolute worst fear, recurring nightmare, and horrific reality come true was that I would become a blob. And for the sake of experientially facing my fears, I embodied this terror, wholly. A blob is fearsome because it is not simply fat. It is immobile. There's no motion to be had. Being a blob is like the process of cultivating fine veal: staying as still as possible while gaining weight. Or, like a goose in the pre-foie gras state, getting fatter and fatter ahead of its own impending death until suddenly, unsuspectingly to the fowl, it explodes.

I woke up one day, and realized I was fat. I had shattered the view of myself I once knew—I had become a blob. There's no other punchline. That's how it happened. I just saw myself, and realized, *Holy cannoli* (nope, can't eat dessert en masse anymore), *I'm outrageously large and I don't recognize myself.* Every cell in my being had stretched in this exploded, unrecognizable, blob-y version of me.

Prior to this wake-up call on a date I can't remember and in a place I've blocked out from my memory, I looked in the mirror and saw the old me. I saw the person I *could* be. I held that vision so strongly that it was actually difficult to see out of my own face. Sometimes, we delude ourselves out of a promise that we match the person we dreamed we could be. It's nefarious because it's so sneaky and subtle.

I found out that transformation starts with accepting the truth. And the honest truth is that I was fat. I couldn't worry it away. I couldn't joke it away. I couldn't run away from the truth; I literally couldn't run, jog, skip, or hop at all anymore without being in severe pain and panting outrageously.

So, I set out on a project to carve Cassie out of the cellulite stone, much like Michelangelo found *David*. I figured I had ripped muscles to find under there, somewhere, deep, deep, deeply hidden in the excess layers of blob-ness that I had acquired along the way. As a part-time sculptor and a part-time painter who uses words to paint on the canvas of life, I decided to chronicle my journey so you would understand how much there is to worry about when you wake up as a blob and decide there's something that must be done about it. Meanwhile, to the leadership of Blobs Anonymous, if you need a spokesperson, I'm available for a fee.

I'd rather live for before-and-after transformation pictures. Whether it's a home remodel, a car remodel, a plastic surgery remodel, a wardrobe remodel, a barn remodel or a weight loss remodel, I'm here for something going from not...to hot. In Australia, the weight loss show that is likened to America's *The Biggest Loser* is affectionately called, *Bringing Sexy Back*. When I embarked, unexpectedly, on my own weight loss journey, I imagined that the worries would subside the more I lost weight and brought my own sexy back. I was in for a ride.

It's well known why one would want to lose weight: to feel better, to look better, to be better. All that self-improvement jazz rings true, certainly. But no one really discusses why it's great to be overweight, at least for a while. If you're a person who balances worry with occasionally looking at the bright side, no matter how dismal your current life might be, I'll give you a few reasons why being overweight is fun. No one's ever told me this, which worries me that everyone's keeping all the fun, fat, juicy secrets of everything to themselves.

The Underrated Benefits of Being Overweight

Alcohol Tolerance

Unbeknownst to skinny, young, cockeyed, twenty-something me, one's alcohol tolerance is in proportion to their height, weight, and genetic dispositions. Scientifically speaking, when my DNA test came back as 40% leprechaun from the west of Ireland, I discovered I can drink more Irish whiskey without becoming inebriated than I can with tequila, for example. Whilst overweight, I could easily down beer, then Korean soju, then more beer all while commanding a plate full of barbecued meat, doing jokes, and later singing karaoke. In other words, I could commit to a full food marathon paired with alcohol while dancing on the table with a tambourine, without falling over or getting kicked out of the karaoke bar. Kids, I'm not saying to do this when you grow up. I'm just saying no one ever told me that while you are overweight, it's time to party. And party, I did. With a standing karaoke ovation.

Clothes Shopping

If you rapidly gain weight, you outgrow all of your clothes. This gives you a perfect chance to go to the store and buy things you never would have bought otherwise, like mysterious and magical underwear and underwire that squish you into a dress a few sizes too small. Or, for the roomier experience, the wardrobe could expand into housing flowy grandma-like muumuus and witness-protection-proof scarves.

I traded in a wardrobe based on jeans and T-shirts for all sorts of flowy and Bohemian garb that I never would have adorned before. While it was expensive and somewhat miserable to try on three or four sizes of jeans before finding the pair that fit, I realized I could ditch jeans forever in favor of skirts and dresses. This launched a multi-year phase in the experimentation of feminine flowy fashion I would have never found without the rapid, uncomfortable, gut-busting weight gain.

One Piece Bathing Suits

The last time I bought a one piece bathing suit was when I went to swim camp at nine years old. Back then, I got to participate in a three-week long summer camp and receive training from Olympic athletes. I competed on a swim team for a year before my hair turned green from the chlorine and I realized I was done with this hobby. At this point, I thought one piece bathing suits were simply to help you slice through the water faster and keep everything "up" and "contained." Turns out, the principle still applies as an adult. And I found I quite liked the one piece bathing suit options. There was less of me to confront in the dressing room mirror, which meant a few less tears. So I donned a new sun uniform and thus entered the phase where my belly did not see the light of day for years at a time. Without those baseline tans each summer, I'm still not sure my tummy zip code will ever recover from the vanilla ice cream white sallow hue.

Glasses

Some people gain weight here or there, in bits and bobs and never full lobs. I'm the kind of person who gains weight everywhere. Which I quite prefer in that it's easier to stuff away and hide the weight gain when your fingers get a pinch, and your ears, and your toes, and your shoe size, and even your nose grow a few centimeters at a time. In an effort to hide my face from the world, which also had gained a substantial amount of weight, I faked eye problems. I had eye insurance. I feel like it's criminal to pay for insurance one does not use. So I went to the eye doctor and told them I had trouble reading.

I'm not illiterate, I told the doctor, "I just need some spectacles." I had 20/25 vision, at best. Truly, I had 20/20 vision but I lied a bit on the test so I could get prescribed some glasses and feel important and scholarly.

I didn't know that the mall sold plain glasses without a prescription, which would have saved me a lot of time, trouble, and humorless optometrist interactions. I had bright ocean blue glasses; fire truck engine red glasses; tortoise shell glasses; and even bold, black, thick-framed glasses. I looked like a gallery curator, a professor, a beatnik, or a magazine editor, depending on the day. They hid me from the world at full-frontal glance, and I was comfortable with this arrangement.

Second Helpings at a Potluck

If you're already overweight, what's one more helping of bacon and jalapeno mac and cheese? Suffering from others saying, "Oh, do you really want more?" with a side-eye glance, I would say, simply, "Yes I do." Then I'd slop another helping of mac and cheese on my plate.

It wasn't an opportune moment to brag about my past athletic life whilst in the food line. Saying, "I might be training for another half marathon soon. In fact, I've completed three in the last few years. Have you run one before?" doesn't make you many friends while vying over casseroles. And it's also hard to enjoy an overindulgence of food when someone is side-eye snobbing your portion choices. The thing is, we're never really one thing or another. Sometimes we're a bunch of things at all at once as humans. It can be a rather messy experience. Sometimes we're fat and loathing and also past athletes and lifetime mac and cheese connoisseurs. Unless you know someone's story, it's hard to judge them by the smorgasbord on their potluck plate.

Dessert

Hello, you elusive minx. I come from a long line of family members who claim, "We're not dessert people." See, in my immediate family, and even the extended relatives who live across town and I see once a year-ish, everyone is thin and healthy. No one has really struggled with obesity. I'm proud to be the rogue black sheep or scientific explorer or method actor, whichever metaphor you approve. If you grow up thinking you're not a dessert person, it's easy to say, "No thanks," and skip it. If you are already overweight, there's little reason to not evaluate the position of being a non-dessert person.

So I made the switch and it was pretty painless at the time. It turns out, addictively sweetened food is really quite appealing, if only for a moment in time. I found a new love of breakfast pastries, fresh French macaroons (which I had never tried), pudding cups (which I bought from the store, in the snack aisle I had previously never visited), and cake.

Cake was the oddest joy to find. I never had cake on my birthday; we'd have something else to celebrate. I don't remember eating cupcakes or cakes growing up. But boy, oh boy, did I find some cakes I really loved from 85°C Bakery Cafe and Paris Baguette, Asian bakery chains in the heart of Koreatown, Los Angeles. 85°C Bakery Cafe is a popular Taiwanese bakery specializing in all sorts of bakery products like egg tarts and fruit custards. Nothing, I mean *nothing*, could be better than a lusciously smooth, custardy egg tart with a steaming cappuccino or an Iced Sea Salt Mountain Green Tea. It's brewed iced tea topped with salted cream cheese foam. The egg tarts, hailing from Taiwan, perfectly imitate the egg tart experience in Portugal. This, my reader friends, is truly internationalism at its finest. In Paris Baguette, I found a Korean French fusion bakery. Éclairs and macaroons are masterfully produced next to red bean and cheese pastries. My favorite is the blueberry yogurt cake—smooth, light, airy, and filled with whipped yogurt filling and blueberry jam. Simply perfection. Turns out my mom enjoyed it one birthday, too. You're welcome, Mom.

Career Highlights

I seemed to skyrocket my career when I gained a lot of weight and became a bit unprepossessing. The more homely I felt, and the more homely I looked, the less it felt I was a threat to others. It was easier to climb the corporate ladder, oddly, when I was overweight because I didn't have to take breaks to work out, or eat five healthy micro-meals a day, or spend time on weekends preparing my meals for the week ahead. I could just autopilot myself as a robotic machine and tear up the business world.

Women were less threatened by me because I was by no means the prettiest person in the room. Men befriended me and sponsored me into better and better roles. It was easier to give and share information with everyone. Being a bit of an ugly duckling was a huge advantage, at least it seemed to be. If you're going to be a scrapper, and punch in a bigger league than your weight class (get it?), having these advantages is helpful.

Pity

If you can't be admired, be pitied. I'm not exactly sure how this benefits you. But in my experience of being overweight, people seem to have a benevolence toward you in such a way that showcases that you're not living up to your potential. Kind souls want to help. So they offer advice. Help. Suggestions. Support. I suppose you can't always be on top in life, so when you're in a valley, it's nice to know people actually care. And when all else fails, just focus on your hair. A good hair day outruns a bad weight day. It's the power of Freudian misdirection.

Upon setting out on my quest to change zip codes from Blob-Ville to Healthy-Town, the very first thing to worry about was figuring out my target healthy weight. I had literally no idea what my goal weight should be. According to the Body Mass Index rating, at 5'2.5" and 168 lbs., I was morbidly obese. First things first, I let that sink in. I cried about it for a while. I ran a scheme for about a month to see if I could cry enough to actually lose weight. I didn't notice a tipping of the scales due to tears cried, for the record.

According to deeper research about the state of obesity in the United States of America, I was pretty average, meaning I possessed a pretty overweight American body type. I wore a size eight or a ten. I watched what I ate, or so I thought. I moved a bit and tried to get my steps in. Maybe my skin wasn't perfectly peachy, my tan was not perfectly beachy. The whites of my eyes were a bit sallow and even a tad yellow, but I ascribed that to looking at a computer screen for too long and not because I ate a bucket of chicken wings to myself at least once a week. I had no intended weight loss goal. I began to worry I might be charting a course without a roadmap.

I have always read that having an accountability partner for weight loss was paramount to your success. I don't know how this whole accountability partnership works, exactly. Do you sign someone up to suffer with and for you to produce a new result in your life? Does anyone actually do that? I *did* enlist a food sponsor, so every day, I told her what I ate. This person should receive a sainthood commendation for having listened to my daily menu week in and week out. These kinds of real, ride-or-die friends exist. They're one in a billion, or less. Other than my menu partner, I set out on this journey alone.

I started really small. I took things at a snail's pace. I decided to measure my steps. I didn't set a goal. As a recovering A-type personality who loves to plan everything and has been known to take a project management approach to running my personal life, I decided to go off script. Walking anywhere, and everywhere, seemed like an appropriate place to start. "Let's see what happens next," I'd say. I found myself even occasionally skipping. I might add that I was in London at this time. It seems easier, somehow, to skip around when you sashay through Kensington Gardens on your way to work. Also, there was some luck involved in choosing a walkable city. It was manageable and possible to walk to work, walk to coffee, walk to the grocery store, walk to the mall, walk to eat, and walk to the pub to perform karaoke on Fridays, etc.

Suspiciously enough, and what seemed against all odds, I ate the same things and walked more, and my clothes started to fit better and better. I worried it was too easy. I spent at least one night lying in bed, awake, counting stars and sheep and thinking, *What if life is easier than what I've been making it?* And the mounting pressure of this thought overwhelmed me. I worried that I had complexified things my whole life. That maybe insipid, imbecile soundbites of advice like "an apple a day" or "walk, don't run" were suddenly rich fodder for a gloriously easier life. This sent me into an existential crisis I have not yet resolved. DO LESS? Impossible. I have letters after my name from a degree no one cares about to prove that I know things about stuff. And what does it all mean, anyway? I started panting, a slight panic breathing reminiscent of a distressed dog. Because being all alone in a foreign country is a perfect time for a meltdown, if you ask me.

I began to worry that "too easy" was too simple. And I wasn't ready to accept this reality. Not in the slightest. So I started phase two, which was prison workouts.

The loneliness of this weight loss journey felt like solitary confinement. I didn't exactly choose to walk this path totally alone at this stage of life, yet it felt a bit like life itself handed me a sentence of solitude. Obviously, imprisoned people know how to make the most of being alone for long stretches of time. I took inspiration from this thought. What would I do if I were the Count of Monte Cristo, imprisoned in a stone castle with all the time in the world to plot revenge? First, I decided I didn't want revenge in a traditional way. I wanted revenge in the way that no matter how life had knocked me down (by my own terrible choices, no less) I could rise again.

For my prison workout series, phase two of weight loss, I started what I called the 250 series. I thrive off of coming up with solutions based on constraints. Me and some scientists seem to agree that, in fact, constraint often provides the most *creative* solutions. The constraints included not owning workout equipment since I was abroad at the time, and living in a three-story flat in London with three other adults (thus, needing to be relatively quiet). Thus, I began a nightly regime of a hundred squats, a hundred crunches, and fifty pushups. I wanted to make it a 300-round series, but after an adult lifetime in front of a computer, my wrists were less compliant than I had hoped. My constraints were also this: I had approximately a 3x5' space. My floor was the ceiling of my landlady's bedroom, so I couldn't be loud. And I needed something I could complete within fifteen minutes or less so I would actually stick to it.

In an ideal world, I thought of myself as the kind of person who woke up early and worked out before work. One day I might wake up and become this person, miracles do happen. But as it turned out, I would sleep in since I had downed a half a bottle of wine or so the night before while discussing philosophy, because that is what one does in Europe, I thought. I was in England, not Europe. It's different and not to be confused. But I would like to be in Europe someday, so I played along.

I kept up with the 250 series for about four months. I would do it right before bed in England, then take a cold shower. I would have ideally preferred a hot shower, but one does not always get what they want in life. I worry it would make me soft if I always indulged. Oh, and the water didn't work well. But I read somewhere that cold showers make you less inflamed. And life is an inflammatory experience, isn't it? A nice, frigid plunge now and again doesn't hurt. I would have kept up with my prison series, but ultimately my wrists started to snap, crack, and pop like a children's cereal and I worried I might have had to amputate.

After phase one of walking around rather aimlessly and stop, drop, and roll prison workouts or fire drills, I had begun to noticeably lose weight. When I had a scale again, after moving back to the United States, I found out I had lost about 20 lbs. in two months. I worried none of my clothes would fit me, but it turned out they fit just fine at this point and even looked better than when I bought them. I had a brief moment of embarrassment realizing just how much weight I had gained from a pattern of work, work, work, and no play (or workouts).

Enter phase three. This was the crossover phase where things really started to get serious.

I started rigorous body weight interval training, high intensity interval training, and paired this with weightlifting and hiking daily. I worry I'll never be a person who eases into things. It's like, "Let's flip a switch and change everything about our life," is more my preferred speed of change. Collateral damage be damned.

My greatest worry in this phase was getting run over by a car. My mission was to find hiking and biking trails where I could zone out in my daydreams and not worry about being pedestrian roadkill. See, the world was still shut down from the global pandemic of COVID-19, so gyms were not an option during this illustrious time of my self-reinvention. I had moved back to Los Angeles. By this time, I had lived in L.A. for a collective fourteen years, and had no idea there were hiking trails around town until I undertook this weight loss journey. To my great joy, I discovered a few hiking trails that had dirt to go under my feet and trees to provide shade, and occasionally were next to a body of water. It's funny what you find out about the world around you when your inner world begins to change. I fell in love with being in nature just moments away from the city, and it felt like a secret garden of escape. Me, and just about everyone else in Los Angeles felt that "right now" was the ideal time to take up hiking whilst imprisoned—errr—confined.

Soon, the trails promptly shut down. For weeks. It was a devastating loss, and I was determined to find a way to keep my positive walking momentum. Next, I carved out a winding pathway amongst suburban tract homes, or what I deemed an urban hiking route. Out my front door, I charted a path straight up the largest hill I could find. I would walk up 1.5 miles and then turn around. Faithfully, every day, I did the same route, just me swinging my arms for extra calorie burn, blasting Hall & Oates on my Apple AirPods, and zooming my bum around blind corners like my life depended on it. My safety protection plan was to jump into the nearest driveway, fence, bush, or pile of trash cans if someone in a car whipped around a corner too fast and I had to boogie out of the way. One time I did have to jump onto the curb because someone's car came close enough to clipping my hip. What's the point of working out if you don't occasionally brush the kiss of death? Further, I was right to worry about getting run over. I knew it was a legitimate concern!

I never deviated from my newly carved route. I think there's something cathartic about trekking the same steps daily when the world around you is out of control. If you can only control your attitude in life, then my attitude suggested it was nice to have one small thing constantly in your life, like your walking route. To this day, I walk the same route daily. I just live in a new place. On day one, I said to my new route, "Hey, I'm Cassie and we're going to be nice friends." There's even a sidewalk this time. I have only been almost hit by a car once, so far.

Back in L.A., one sunny day, I decided to do more than my allotted 1.5 mile urban hiking route. This was allowable and still in the vein of keeping the same route for your sanity, but it is a bit weird to step outside the known boundaries. I followed the road up just a few houses past where I would normally stop and realized I was on Mulholland Drive. I crossed over just a few hundred feet and saw the expansive valley of Los Angeles sprawling out beneath my toes. I had a 180-degree view, the best in the city, just by plopping myself down on the side of the road. Comfortably perched on the road embankment, this became my sunset viewing post. Occasional dance spot. Thinking place. Yoga salutation arena. I nearly never found my now favorite place in Los Angeles because of my rigid routing techniques. I worry I'm not enough of a risk taker, sometimes.

In phase three, walking continued to be paramount to my success. I logged three miles daily, rain or shine. Lockdown or freedom. Sidewalks or trails or blazing my own path. I started to feel really good. I saw myself in the mirror and began to like what I saw. To enhance the process of inner transformation, I assumed a challenge to tell myself, "I love you," in the mirror ten times a day. But ten times was asking too much most days. I could consistently get up to three times before I started to cry and gave up. This took me weeks. Maybe months. At that time, even a small smile of self-approval or self-gratitude would do.

As aforementioned, I love remodels. I live for transformations and side-by-side comparison photos of before and afters. Then-and-now photos are so dreamy. I took many, many photos of myself. I have an ungodly amount of selfies on my phone. In my defense, point one, no one else was around or available to take my photo. In my defense, point two, I set out on the weight loss journey to learn to respect and love myself more. Seeing myself from different angles was enlightening. Recording this time in my life became self-study in so many ways.

I did occasionally share these self-portraits with a few close girlfriends. For as many people who cheered me on, there were a few folks who kindly told me that I looked good in the "before" photo and they didn't know why I was trying to lose weight. I was initially worried about the shameless self-promotion, but I hadn't realized how to worry about the reaction to the photos. I was honored to have people in my life who loved me regardless of my size, but when I was sitting at approximately 60 lbs. overweight at a mere 5'2.5" stature, I was shocked that anyone would think I looked good then. I hadn't wondered or worried that people might prefer me bigger. Or, that folks would question my choice to lose weight. It never occurred to me to realize that some people prefer you to stay the same—a blob—rather than proceed into the great unknown of what you could become.

Body acceptance is on the rise, and yet I wasn't feeling very accepted by some of my more progressive gal pals. I worry we've gone too far as a culture to say that anything goes. By saying, "Be anything you want," or, "Do anything you want," I wonder if we've lost direction a little bit. A social contract is predicated on there being rules of engagement. It actually doesn't work for anyone to do *anything* they want *anytime* they want to. Take arson, as a key example. Smokey Bear is against wildfires y'all. Whose right is it, anyway, to live their best bear life? Striking a match to each one's fantasy without consequences is sillier than a bear getting their hand stuck in a jar of honey.

Realizing that some folks might cheer me on and some folks might prefer not to hear anything about my weight loss journey gave me pause. When we undertake massive self-growth and self-change efforts, not everyone will be in our courts. Some people in our lives love us just as we are today, and they want us to stay the same. Some people in our lives love us and want us to be more like them. Some people in our lives love us and see themselves in us, which is either good, bad, or ugly, depending on the day.

I had a hair-brained idea around this time to post my weight loss transformation photo publicly on the Internet to see if I could become insta-famous. This didn't work in respect to gaining followers. But it did seem to cure my fear of public embarrassment. Now instead of imagining me as an audience member in my underwear, there's a picture that essentially replicates that online.

And yes, nothing can be deleted, truly. I guess I feel a little more exposed and simultaneously a little less scared, and I did it in the name of scientific exploration.

I wondered how it would feel to embark on a change of this magnitude as a solitary endeavor. I genuinely believed in the past I could do more and be more in relationship to others. If I supported them, they'd support me. It's kind of like quid-pro-quo kindness. If I show up and do this workout with you, then you will show up someday for me. I've been exchanging fitness favors for almost a decade. I even ran three half marathons in my early twenties because someone close to me wanted to become a runner. I'm not even sure to this day if I like running or not, but I logged hundreds of training miles just to prove I was the kind of friend who showed up.

So, who did I become when there was no one looking and no one to prove anything to? Everyone asks me, "What's the ONE thing you did that made all the difference?" People want one tip. One answer. I tell them, to this day: love.

I just lost weight and loved myself more. And loved myself more which made me lose more weight. It was so simple. Love was the key ingredient. Plus two hour daily workouts and walking three miles a day.

Phase four began with me realizing I was down about 35 lbs. but exhausted and burned out. It's not normal to cry over your bowl of oatmeal while dreading a day of workouts you planned for yourself. The thing is, oatmeal tastes better if you add a pinch of salt. Usually the pinch of salt is not in the form of a saline tear reduction. I had to make a change. I had to learn how to face my day with courage and conviction. And crying over my oatmeal every day was getting really old for me. I needed to create another well-being set point, somewhere else to diffuse my attention away from the pain of muscle gain.

At the point where you lose enough weight where your clothes no longer fit, it's time to purge the wardrobe. If life was neat rather than messy, I would have donated my clothes to a thrift store, like an upstanding citizen. However, I felt the old me embodied in this clothing stack needed a more dramatic ending; a final, fabulous finale, if you will. And the last thing I wanted was to keep hallmarks and harbingers of my past life skulking around like skeletons of my former self. I did the only self-respecting thing I could—I ripped and shredded the clothing piece by piece. It was one of the most liberating things I had done. Physically, I had been shedding weight for months. The clothes that reminded me of the past? I took scissors to the seams and ripped them apart with my bare hands. Then, I took out the trash.

Some conservationists in my life wondered what had become of my old wardrobe. "I trashed it," I'd say. Agasp, they asked, how could I do such a thing? "Well, one load at a time into the trash can," was my easy answer. Sometimes simple is best.

Enter phase five. High intensity training and rapid weight loss left me exhausted, if not somewhat skinnier and significantly happier about how I looked. I realized, however, if I wanted this to be a lifestyle change instead of a Band-Aid solution to a multi-year addiction to junk food, overworking, and complexification, I needed to shift my focus to sustainability.

I struck a new chord on the tune of my life revival and changed to barre class. Blending ballet, yoga, and Pilates, barre class was a new foray into the mix of strength and grace. I fell on my literal arse a lot during this phase. I would have beads of sweat plummeting off my face at a faster rate than high intensity training, but on the surface, it looked like I was moving a micro-fraction of an inch. I worried such a short, small series of workouts would be ineffective. Wrong. I thought I could never find a workout that made my soul sing. Wrong. I mean, it occasionally sang with expletives as I reached and toddled and tried to find my balance. But, cultivating a sense of inner peace and balance while learning to move with my body in a way that no longer resembled prison yard recess seemed like a fitting new phase.

The thing is, I realized no one is overly interested in what I do for workouts. Even when they ask, "How did you lose weight? How are you staying active during confinement? Why haven't you atrophied into a blob from binging TV?" (Easy, I don't watch TV except on Sundays, which is also when I crave, and can't eat, Chick-fil-A). And, even when they mean well by asking and even exhibit vague interest, their eyes glaze over when I tell them the truth. It's about love. And two-hour daily workouts. But mostly, love.

Truly, the only person who cares to tell me how things are going is my gay best friend. They will tell me when I looked bad (I did) and when I look good now (I do). And that I'll look better soon when I hit goal weight (I will). They send me kiss emojis without expectations of anything "happening" and heart all my photos. And they'll tell me this to my face, without even gossiping behind my back. I like this direct honesty.

For me, the point of working out is not really about looking better, although that's a happy side note. I really wanted to be able to do activities. What kind of activities, you ask? Well, anything that came to mind. I wanted to actually do something with my body considering I had lost weight. What's the point of the weight loss journey if you're not able to move your new body around and train for the circus?

Hence, phase six: horseback riding and tennis lessons.

Sometimes life gives you metaphors, like getting back on the horse. Sometimes I take them literally, and so I began horseback riding lessons at age thirty-one.

There's something cathartic and humbling about being a total beginner at anything after you've spent a life trying to prove you're good at things. What things? Any things. Things that come up. Things that other people want you to be good at. Things you think you should be good at.

About fifteen or so years ago, I was the type of person who tried a new activity, and if I wasn't "good" at it the first time, I'd quit. I don't think of myself as a quitter, per se. I think I've just stuck with odd things for reasons that weren't joy-filled. What I realized is that now I'd like to be open to not having to be good at something in order to find joy in it. In order to find growth in myself while trying a new activity, I decided to become willing to have a humble beginner's mindset.

To get clear on what I want this season in life to feel like, I decided to invite a space of perpetual summer camp. I want to feel as if I have arrived in a nurturing, curious place where it is safe to try new activities. Where every day holds a sense of adventure. When it feels as if many things are possible. Where you meet people with stories as the primary vehicle of truth-telling, developing deep bonds and a sense of true togetherness. There's a mess hall. Crisp air. Every night you gaze at the stars and hear their star songs.

Yes. What I want my life to feel like is summer camp.

So, I've been designing it to be so. What one can imagine, one can create.

Brief disclaimer: I'm the busiest person you know who does nothing. A moment of reflection: even in doing "nothing," it's hard for me not to do "something." And it's hard for me to not have a schedule, even if the schedule is penciling in existential meltdowns now and again, which include crying and stomping for a while as I actively expel my thoughts and get into my body to feel whatever I need to feel. The feeling the feelings process is not just for emotional fitness—I didn't want stuck feelings to turn into cellulite. The alternative of not feeling was what I tried for years, and that simply did not work. It's much better to plan to cry and then not use your cry date than accidentally cry at inappropriate times.

I love to be studious even if there is no grade to achieve. Self-improvement is actually one of my oldest pursuits, just ask my childhood best friend. I used to wake us up at 5:00 a.m. so we could use pastels with our left hands to illustrate the sunrise. We're both right-handed but I read once that to connect to your right brain and induce more creativity, you have to use the left side of your body. We were about nine years old for our sunrise pastel pursuits. At sixteen years old, the first place I went with my driver's license was the public library. Literacy is liberation. My romantic fantasy at that age (and, thus far, unfulfilled) was to be asked on a learning date or to read the same books as my boyfriend and discuss them in detail. "Hey girl, wanna learn stuff?" never really caught on as an Internet meme. I wonder why.

So, getting back on the horse...

The very, very first lesson in horseback riding: situational awareness.

The first thirty seconds of my lesson entailed my no-nonsense teacher running me down all the ways I could get bucked, maimed, kicked, or otherwise bodily harmed. She said, "You need to be aware of everything that could go wrong at every second and have a plan." I wanted to retort, "I've been divorced twice by the tender age of thirty, moved abroad all alone, quit my executive job with zero plans, have tried (and failed) to start many companies, and learned to exist while gainfully unemployed..." And that was just a brief recap of the first half of 2020. Of all folks I know, I know that I have had a lesson in prepping for life gone awry. If everything in my life had gone "right" then I wouldn't have any material to write this book, in fact. I'd be bland. Boring. In response to my horse trainer, I merely shook my head, and nodded knowingly. I do wonder if anyone else feels like their life has been a course in situational awareness as keenly as I have felt mine is.

Here's what I am learning in the equestrian arena, also affectionately known as the...

Annie Oakley Phase

Ask. Make. Tell. To move forward: first, squeeze. Second, light tap. Third, kick. The horse knows this progression and will test my aptitude and follow through to see what quality of rider I am (a novice, initiate, beginner...). Reflecting on myself, asking in general has been hard. Asking for what I want, asking for what I need...hard. I think this is already an important lesson. I need to ask. Asking is step one.

I am in charge. I am the boss. There's a natural hierarchy. *I'm in charge.* The horse is trained to follow me. I've been a leader and I've been a follower. I've remembered my power and I've forgotten it. This is a remembering season.

Ask. It's up to me to ask for what I need. *Ah.* Back to the asking. I have a need—to go forward, to stop, to turn...to go fast, to slow down, to ease up... I need to be aware of how I need to give clear directions. This feels more and more like therapy by the minute.

Free your pelvis, free your mind. Hips need to move and flow with the horse. The somatic philosopher, Shakira, knowingly said that the hips don't lie. And I don't think they do, either. You can't hide on the horse. And your hips are the gateway into comfort, control, confidence. (I think I'm learning more than one lesson at a time.)

How to stop a 1,000-pound animal with your breath alone... I exhale and breathe out fully to stop the horse. My favorite part of the lesson is learning how to stop the horse merely with my breath and a nice cat-like c-curve in my back. Inhaling broadly, exhaling deeply, and settling into an exaggerated c-curve with my heels up, the horse comes to a complete stop. I am always mesmerized. How many times are we giving the universe either clear or mixed signals with our breath and our way of being?

It's okay to be a beginner. There's humility in starting from scratch. I used to be the kind of person who wouldn't try something if I wasn't good at it from the starting line. I've selected two hobbies now (tennis and horseback riding) that are inherently difficult to master without years of study. I feel like I'm in humility school and I'm going to get all the value I can out of being a beginner with a day one mindset.

My learning continues. The worst injury so far I've sustained is my sternum slamming into the saddle horn and nearly knocking me out of breath. I lived to breathe another day.

It's hard to know if this is therapy learning or equestrian learning, but so far, I've come away from the ranch with a few life lessons, if not with my full dignity intact (I embarrass myself regularly).

Life Lessons Learned While Horsing Around

Make a plan. The horse is expecting me to have a plan. Confidence comes with having a plan and curiosity comes when the plan needs improvisation.

Keep my eyes on the horizon. There is no reason to look at the horse when riding, other than to see their eyes, which will tell you the quality of their energy and are the window into their soul. To stay grounded, keep a broader view: look at the horizon. Know the environment and pulse with the bigger picture.

Talk with my body, not words. "No verbal commands," my trainer tells me when I ask the horse to go. *Okay. This is a new language.* Despite growing up dancing, I've largely forgotten as an adult what it means to speak with my body and tell a story with my movements and energy rather than using words. Words can be a weapon, words can be a screen, but the body energy cannot lie. And the horse knows that. There is no hiding. Who you really are, and the quality and condition of your energy will come out. This feels special and important to realize and remember.

Balance. All of my balance is giving direction and giving information away about my state of being. The goal is not perfect balance but swift recovery. I think I can jive with this part of the lesson. Makes sense, but I want to put it into motion and put this knowledge into my cells. It's not enough to think about it. It's not enough to feel it. It has to be lived in motion.

Eye contact, always. What's the best way to get to know my horse? Eye contact.

Everything is a test. There's a lot of life that's a tad easier to accept when you realize it's all a test. And most tests are not graded, they are usually pass/fail. And failure is just as good of a teacher, if not a more sage one.

Be worthy. I have to assert my worthiness. Again, this feels more like a life lesson. *I deserve to be here, I am here, and I am worthy to be here.* To embody this fully will open up more experiences for me on the horse. And, in life.

Part deux of CampCass™ is tennis lessons.
It's a miracle, an anomaly of time and fate, if I arrive anywhere on time. I'm mystified. Overjoyed. Astounded. My timing in life always seems to be on a rhythm all to myself, and I'm not sure anyone else shares my pace. To give you a strong idea of what I mean by saying I live in my own world on my own time, I present to you an exhibit from experience: getting a ticket for going too slow and accidentally running a red light.

The scene is set in Beverly Hills. The characters are me, my second Camry named Carmen, and a blinking, bright white light that captured my mug shot across the intersection. There was no human interaction in the making of this ticket.

When I went down to the police station to arrange for payment, the very nice lady in blue told me, "Sweetie, we just don't see this very often. But you're *under* the speed limit." She looked into my eyes and told me she knew I meant well and was trying my best.

Continuing on, she offered me an invite: to come back to the station any time another ticket tripped me up. I nodded, quietly, knowing I didn't want to get too friendly at a police station. But I do have my apologetic posture and slight Southern twang down just in case I need to appear more contrite than usual. I said "ma'am" a lot and looked shy, which I think was received well since I look younger than I really am. This will only work for so long, I know that, y'all (said long and syrupy).

The truth is, I got the red light ticket because I was thinking about stuff, alone in my own little world, while trying to operate heavy machinery in L.A. rush hour. $750 later, being on my own time clock was terribly expensive. FutureCass™ has solved this whole car business by acquiring a driver. I hope to meet both FutureCass™ and the driver real soon.

CampCass™ has a fairly rigorous schedule, if for no other reason than to prepare material for writing a book, or to have material for stand-up jokes at cocktail parties. And gosh darnit, I try to get to every lesson on time.

Here's what I'm learning in tennis lessons, trademarked courtesy of CampCass™:

Serve it right up. The serve starts the game and is also a temperature check of athletic ability, precision, timing, and strategy. It feels like something I should learn to nail and nail it hard. I mean, without sounding aggressive, why would I take up a sport and not try to smash it? The hardest thing for me to begin with is aim. I don't have the best depth perception, in general, and aiming at a target is hard work. To make this more complicated, I have to toss the ball with my left hand and time my swing. "Have you ever played contact sports with balls before?" my coach asked. This was hard to answer. I smirked and said no. "Why not?" he asked. I said, "Because I don't want balls to hit me in the face."

Don't take off early. We're back to timing here, y'all. Apparently, my lack of a life clock translates a bit to the game of tennis, too. I'm often not late, and while in lessons, I don't miss the ball very often. But I do jumpstart the clock an awful lot. Afraid to miss, I spike a shot earlier than I should. Suspiciously, I am instructed to do this thing called "trust" and "feel it," which sounds nonsensical to me. But I'm trying. I'm keeping an open mind. I usually arrive at the ball too early and reach too far. I think I've felt this way a lot of times in my life. I want to use up the minutes and months and moments as early and as much as possible, and PastCass™ has definitely jumped the gun. I'm willing to imagine becoming the type of person who can flow with time and let things come to her.

Cross my body. Most of the footwork in tennis requires a cross-body step. I lose my balance when I have to cross my body. Like a crab, I feel better side-to-side. I'm not sure yet what this says about me as a person, but I know if I think hard enough about Jungian archetypes again, something will arise in my dream state and I might have to kill a metaphorical wild boar with a unicorn horn.

I have a follow-through issue. This feels personal, like tennis is attacking my character, here. I have to just come out and say it straight: I have a follow-through issue. You can't hide in sports, either. Which is why I prefer books, obviously. After two grueling lessons, I have matched a pattern for me and tennis swings: I don't follow through, even though I want to. But I stop after I strike the ball. And I sit there dumbfounded because I want to do better and swing thoroughly, but I just don't. I have a follow-through issue. I'm supposed to practice this in front of the mirror without putting the racket through the mirror. I hope the moment I manage to break the pattern of the lack of follow-through is *not* the same moment I break the mirror, as that would be terrifically unlucky.

Less power, more technique. Might makes right, no? I thought if I trained my butt off and became super strong and lifted weights and ran and did barre and ran and biked and hiked and paddle boarded and swam and did a zillion other activities like I have been doing for months, that I'd finally be strong enough to hit stuff hard, which was a desired third activity to my pipeline of things to stay active.

My focus has been to learn proper technique so that power will complement my smooth moves. I am saddened to learn I cannot muscle through bad technique. I want to hit and hit hard. But right now I'm supposed to focus on wrist mobility and grace.

Little movements, more meaning. Less full expression, more intentionality with my motions. This seems feasible but still annoying. I like big. I like bold. I like to go where I'm told not to roam. But I'm literally paying someone to tell me exactly what to do to get better, so I'm really trying my best to listen. Making meaning with my body movements feels like a skill I'd love to learn from dance, from tennis, from being in the world in an embodied way. I'm committed to trying, or at least *trying* to try which feels like step one.

I'm not afraid to fail + fully commit. Especially early on, coaches are complementary because they want you to keep paying for services, so says CautiousCass™. What was noted in my first and second lessons is that I'm not afraid to fully commit to my swing, even if I end up missing the ball. Other players will take less "good" shots in favor of more ball contact. I'm showing up, fully ready and in literal full swing, even if there's no chance I'll hit the ball. I'm not sure how this is a good thing, but I'm taking the coach at his word that it's a good posture to maintain. The truth is, I'm becoming less afraid of failure, the more experience I have under my belt. I think I'm more afraid to fully live and set my soul on fire. I worry the fear of what could go right occasionally outweighs my encyclopedic knowledge of what could go wrong.

Take the game forward. The whole objective of tennis is to move the game forward; you're always advancing. A popular phrase in business is "burn the ships." This means that when you land somewhere, you torch your arrival vessel so the crew knows there is no turning around, the only option is to move forward. Sun Tzu puts it this way: *"Victorious warriors win first then go to war, while defeated warriors go to war first then seek to win."* I'd like to have some more wins in my life. I'm opening myself up to them. Right now, I consider CampCass™, in general, a giant win.

Immersed in the game of tennis, in the sun, in stretching myself to learn new things, in actively living a daydream, I realized I am finally on time for a life by my own design. I've learned how to take up space and live my life fully. Perhaps for the first time.

My weight loss journey was about making the time count, not counting the time. I told myself this on repeat. Sometimes you believe your own material, and other times you just make jokes. Hopefully my life isn't one of the jokes. For now, I'm focused on having fun.

The real insane summary of this insanely long chapter is I've learned to do less. Love more. That's it. That's the secret to weight loss.

Do less of the things that harm, like overeating, under-sleeping, not moving, and generally hating every second of the life you created. Do less striving. Do less powerful movements that exert rather than extend your well-being and mobility. Do less thinking; leave more time for wonder and exploration.

And ultimately, love more. Love yourself more. Love your life more. Love your body more. Love your blood enough to drink plenty of water to oxygenate it. Love your organs and muscles enough to eat the food that promotes growth and regrowth. Love your cells enough to think nice thoughts toward them, too. They replicate rapidly on your behalf all the time, or so science says.

And, don't wait for the world to congratulate you. Don't worry what they'll say or think. None of us know who "they" are, anyway. We never have and we never will.

But what's real? What's real is that you can make any change you want to make, even on the scale. I did so against registered medical advice. No joke. Years ago, my doctor told me I was overweight. (I already knew that, but thank you.) "It's a bummer to be overweight," she said, "but it's hard to change, so you might as well not try." She gave me a pamphlet for a weight loss support group and mentioned that due to chemistry when we get fat, our bodies don't like to lose weight. "So it'll be an uphill battle to lose weight and most people don't win, but if you want to try, you can go ahead. Or not." (She said that, too). I crumpled in momentary defeat on the exam table; she just kept on talking about how I would likely be fat my whole life. Bedside manner for the win. But, with love, I proved her wrong.

H ere's the world's shortest summary on what to worry about when you're fat:

You might not enjoy it while it is happening. You might lose weight before you really think about how much fun you were having while being fat. Then, you've missed out on the whole entire point of gloating in the goodness before it melts away.

As described at the beginning of the chapter, here's my before and after transformation picture in less than 1,000 words:

Life is easier when you're pretty and thin. People like you more. They don't always get to know what's down beneath the surface, but you can easily glide through life with the pleasure of being publicly palatable. This might not even be a good goal. Have you met the general public recently?

Life might get deeper when you gain weight. You have to actually work to show your personality, your humor, your wit, and your wisdom. People will make snap judgments about you based on the way you look, so you have to open up your inner life more than might be comfortable to give them a more multidimensional picture.

Some people will prefer the old you. They'll prefer you when you eat a bucket of chicken wings and a tray of cupcakes with them while watching reality television for hours. They'll prefer that you go out drinking and then sleep all the next day and miss moments of your life due to the extended food coma. They'll prefer the hangover brunch version of you downing a bloody mary and eating a heaping plate of waffles with melted butter and enough bacon that you could resemble a full piglet.

Some people will celebrate you. Keep them around. Cheer them on, too. It's fun to be better, together.

Some people will be insanely jealous of you. Some people won't believe you, even after seeing your before and after pictures. Forget about them. There's still a few billion people around the world who might want to be friends with you.

Everyone is carrying around private weight they don't talk about. Having been thin, fat, healthy, unhealthy, diseased, depressed, athletic, well and vibrant, I've really enjoyed a multiplicity of seats on the scale of life. What I do know, and I worry we don't collectively remember enough, is that everyone carries a tremendous amount of weight in their own personal story. Thick, thin, or anywhere in between, every human has a universe of cells that are their own, individual, uniquely held bundle of truth.

Every single person I meet who knows I once lost 50 lbs. will ask me my secret, as if there's knowledge I possess that only I know about weight loss. No one ever believes me when I tell them the truth: that when I worried less about other people loving me, and started to love myself, everything changed. I was able to eat balanced, walk more, dance lighter, and live brighter.

There's nothing inherently woo-woo about self-love. It's the simple practice of accepting your own personhood and saying you belong on this planet. That you deserve to take up space. That you matter. That your story and your cells are important. It's a posture of practice—one that says you're willing to engage in life as a full contact sport, not sit on the sidelines as a spectator, heckler, or ticket scalper. You're in the game. If you put yourself in the game with love, you win sometimes. And you lose sometimes. We're not meant to be static. Motion is medicine. Being in motion is living—if you need a point to it all, that's it.

So, where'd I end up? I worried you'd never ask.

I lost 50 lbs. I kept it off. I gained 3-5 lbs. a couple of times around the holidays or while on vacation, but I had every tool in my toolbox to come back to a healthy, aligned weight.

Here's what else I gained: self-respect, self-love, self-confidence. I gained muscle. I lost fat. I trimmed things and tightened the skin up, but more importantly...I danced. I breathed. I rested when I needed to. I drank a lot more water. I ate fresher things. I finished a 10k run. I moved my body every day in some way that was delightful, and in some training ways that were momentarily painful—and those moments, too, passed.

Eventually, I looked in the mirror and could say "I love you"—

not just ten times in a row, but whenever I captured my own gaze. We never see our own faces, just a reflection. Isn't that amazing? And when I see the reflection of what my face must look like to others, I decided it is worth smiling about. Not a small smirk, but a big, toothy, bright, full-out grin.

I no longer think about the weight I lost. I think about how every time I see my reflection, there's something I can find to be happy about. There's a person there who I found abundant, deep love toward.

As for me and myself? We're working on building a friendship, too; sometimes it's slow-going because she is so wordy. It's hard to get a sentence in every now and again.

Against all odds—and despite being a bit odd myself—I've learned that sometimes you can, in fact, tip the scales in your favor. Sometimes, things *do* go right. Sometimes, love wins. And it is, in fact, possible to live a life you love. Even if you don't recognize yourself sometimes. Even if you don't recognize the world around you, sometimes. Even if you change in such a positive way, you know there's no going back to the way things once were.

The truth is, I believe in you to make these positive changes in your life, too.

Chapter 11

Let's Worry about Romantic Relationships and Food

Have you ever been in love? The kind of full-body connection where all of your senses turn from dull to distinctly "on"? Tumbling forward into the emotionality of connection, you are fast in, head over heels. Yet, you stay grounded, somehow, in the very present moment you are experiencing because *now* is the most real time there ever was and might ever be. The type of feeling you get that you are cozily comfortable, utterly at home, positively relaxed, even when venturing into unknown territory. Elation mixed with curiosity. Mystery unraveling as you find connection through conversation, storytelling, and laughter. The ability to drop your veil and reveal more and more of who you truly are when you discover yourself, anew, through the eyes of another. The articulation of true, sumptuous, sensual pleasure in just the right proportions at just the right time.

All that stuff above? Well, that's how I feel about a good meal.

Relationships themselves are a lot like the concert of cooking. There is a preparation phase. Things, like stories and values, need to be picked and parsed and put into clearly marked containers for examination. Sourcing is important—where are you getting the ingredients? Are you farm fresh and au naturel or are you a big box store goer? The instruments are sharpened. Are you able to argue well? Do you communicate clearly? Roles are established. Who does what? Who takes out the trash? Who plans the activities? Who pays? The supporting cast is important. Are you friends with their friends? When do you meet their family? There are moments of heightened energy and anxiety, like meal service. And there are times of calmness, like a shot of cognac after the kitchen is wiped clean. Ebbs and flows. Famine and feasting. Adrenaline and equilibrium. Transitions and tranquility. If you want to test drive a new relationship, try cooking together.

Here's what to worry about if you embark on a romantic evening in with two chefs:

Take the Wheel of Cheese

Someone has to take charge. No matter how egalitarian you are, someone needs to take the lead. Speaking as someone who has historically grasped and gripped for control, it is absolutely amazing when someone steps up with a plan and swoops in with a way to execute it. Speaking for fierce and free women everywhere, nothing is better than giving up control to someone who is adept at actually doing things in the kitchen. One of my favorite quotes is that women *do* belong in the kitchen...with a glass of wine and their feet on a stool being luxuriously listened to and fabulously fed. If you are partnering in the kitchen with the kind of person who has a million questions about what to do next, like, "What do you think is the best way to cook this?" Or if they can't execute a decision on their own? Run. If you're in the kitchen with someone who can't read and follow a simple step-by-step recipe? Run. If you are in the kitchen with someone who says, "I don't know what I feel like, what do *you* feel like?" and puts every question back on you? Run. People other than you need to be able to plan. Otherwise it's not an equal partnership. "I have no ideas; I just want to hear your ideas." Baloney. And I'd rather eat a bologna sandwich than listen to that.

Course Correction: Ordering In

Perhaps the meal has gone south and the only resource to ingest the requisite daily calories is to order in. This could be forgivable. But if someone cannot execute a meal, how are they supposed to execute a relationship? I get that I'm going to get a lot of flack for this comment, but you should be able to follow the simplest directions on a recipe. If you cannot do this, how can you plan a vacation? Build your career? Manage your personal finances? It's highly suspect. If someone cannot cook, I'm just saying, take a second glance around for other tell-tale signs of future ineptitude. Food is the kind of thing you have daily, even multiple times a day if you're really lucky. If you cannot get good at feeding yourself, how are you supposed to feed me? Hunger isn't my best look, and neither is patience. We all have our self-growth journeys to endure.

Is Sharing Caring?

Whenever I go out to eat, my preferred plan would be to 1) eat at a small plate restaurant where you can try as many things as possible or 2) split at least two dishes with my dining partner. If we're at brunch, it's a must to order something sweet and something savory and split both dishes. How am I supposed to get my salt and protein fix to balance me out while devouring the custard brioche French toast with bourbon banana glaze if we're not also sharing the California eggs Benedict with thick cut bacon and avocado slices? Sharing is caring. Dividing and conquering is key. If someone is unwilling to share a meal, this is suspicious to me. I don't even have to know or like you to ask you to split something with me. The worst offense was when I asked my coworker for one-third of her Yerba Mate energy drink, because I was mildly addicted at the time. I figured asking for half was too much, so I reduced the ask. She still said no but I'm just saying, sharing is caring. While cooking together, look for signs of generosity. Ensure tasting spoons are used and then discarded. It's too soon when you're early on in the dating relationship to double dip your taste testing spoon. If kitchen cleanliness and food sanitation skills are questionable, run. Even better, require your partner to show you their Food Handlers Safety Card before endeavoring upon this shared cooking experience. It only costs $8 online for five years and it will provide them the knowledge of the correct temperatures for cooking meat. Essential.

Sharpen the Skills

I am not saying this out of judgment, but isn't dating an elongated interview process? Check to see what skills are being used in the kitchen. Can you work with a knife? Are you dextrous? Can you manage multiple things at one time? How is your timeliness? These are all critical components to managing a relationship. If someone cannot chop vegetables, I question their motor skills. If they cannot keep a watch on the time while pouring wine and making conversation, then I question the capacity for them to manage their own life timing and career without my coaching interference. If they are showing off, then I question their self-confidence. If they are doing anything less than being Emeril Lagasse and kicking it up a notch, I'm not even sure why we're here.

Vocalize the Plan

How do you two communicate in the kitchen? This is a metaphor for your future life together. If things get terse and tense while the literal heat is on, run. You can do better. If they cannot explain what comes next and give directions in a sane, safe, satisfying manner, run. If they are demanding and demanding about your skills or lack of skills, run. This is supposed to be a date. And dating is supposed to be fun. I mean, people say it is, anyway.

Atmosphere Matters

If there are no candles, flowers, artful plates, atmospheric music, and cloth napkins, then I'd rather eat alone, at home. The thing is, I do all of that romantic stuff for myself every day. I wish I had more to say here, but I'm keeping this one really crisp, clean, down to brass tacks, and bottom line.

Cue the Dance Break

Time to get metaphysical. If the joy is solely in the destination and you're not stopping to slow dance in the kitchen while the sauce simmers, then I'm not sure what the point is. I can spin myself in the kitchen doing pirouettes while producing food all day, every day, alone, and I do. If you can't stop to smell the roses (which you most definitely have on the counter) and aren't taking the time to enjoy doing life with someone else, what's the ever-living point to it all? You would be better off on a stage of one where you can choose the music and the menu.

Cooking together feels optimal on a few levels: promoting teamwork, defining communication styles, and keeping the carb-to-cocktail ratio in a healthy position. Faced with the choice of liquid calories or non-liquid calories, I say choose the path that leads you to hydration nation. Beautiful boozy martini or bountiful breadbasket? No contest.

There's a relationship red flag that I'd like to clue you in for your well-being and gladness. It's subtle, and feels warm and cozy at first. But it'll creep up on you if you let it. The sinister availability of food delivered to your doorstep is a decay waiting to rot your relationship. I congratulate everyone who has figured out how to make delivery service exist in the world. But no one is talking about how it will ruin your happiness if you over-exercise the privilege. If you and your boo do find that you're ordering in more and more, ask yourself why. What's gone wrong?

Here's what to worry about if you order in too often:

Spending Time to Define "Too Often"

If you need to have a conversation to determine if you're ordering in too often, have a defensive posture while reading this sentence, or tell me that there's no such thing as "too often," you are ordering in too often. The definition is in the name, here.

Looks Can Be Deceiving

Perhaps you order in because your partner is embarrassed about how you look. This is awkward, but I'm going there. Maybe you're embarrassed about how *they* look. Maybe they are overprotective and believe no one should look at your pretty face. Or, they just truly hate eye contact with strangers. Either way, I've planted the seeds of doubt. But isn't that better than living in a daydream? At any rate, examine how looks can be deceiving, or perhaps looks are telling you all you need to know.

Bad Table Manners

If you eat sushi off of chopsticks at home, you might lose your edge. The problem with never going outside is you might forget how to behave when you re-emerge into the general population. While the gen pop might not have the best table manners, I'd like to imagine mine are fairly good. Poor table manners, however, are a real turn-off. If you imbibe and ingest too much delivery food at home, just remember to consider how your manners, like muscles, might atrophy and wither away and die. Soon you could be grunting and pointing instead of articulating and gesticulating.

We Only Speak during Commercial Breaks, So Streaming Means We Don't Talk at All

While rest and digest is our natural default, not fight or flight, it is questionable if our bodies are truly designed for vegetation. If we were the type of organism that could photosynthesize, then I think the television should project sunlight and we could functionally eat whilst ingesting media. Media could then become even more meaningful as a source of physical substance, nourishing the body simultaneously to numbing the mind. Eating in front of the television is how my dad mentioned his family avoided all conversation and conflict during their formative years. I'm wondering if the repeated habit of delivering food and discovering which episode to auto-play next as a default habit might also be a mechanism for misery—the subtle kind that sneaks up on you with major dissatisfaction, but it won't slap you in the face. Perhaps this is just something to consider.

Compound Interest of Delivery Fees

Imagine for a moment if you had invested your delivery fees

rather than receiving food at your front door. Let's pretend you're the kind of person who might have spent $800 eating out per month. Is that gross? Yes, maybe. If your delivery fees are 10% of the total money spent, that's $80/month. Invested at 6% interest, that would yield $1,044.80 per year. Over five years, that would be $5,518.67. Can you really afford not to drive to pick up your own chicken wings? Just asking for a friend.

Battle Royale: Hawaii vs. Delivery Food

Once upon a time, I was young and had limited income. I was neither destitute nor a debutante. I was squarely average. It was the "before" times. Before the Internet of things, of which things I don't really understand. Way, way back then, I didn't have an application on my phone that would bring tasty treats and appetizing items directly to my doorstep. I shopped at a produce store that sold nearly ripe (read: rotten) goods to save money. I made rice and beans in a rice cooker while on vacation so I didn't have to buy food. I mean, I took "thrift" to a very next level. And, because of all the pennies pinched, even on a tiny fraction of an income, I managed to take myself to Hawaii for a week as a young twenty-something. The thing is, I would later spend a boatload of money on takeout and not go to Hawaii. My effective per hour rate might have been higher later on, but the happiness of the money in some ways did not stretch quite as far. To put it clearly, I chose eating sushi weekly instead of eating sushi yearly in Hawaii. One is not inherently better than the other. But I think it's an interesting point of contrast and reflection due to the fact that the ingestion of delivery food was at an inverse curve against happiness. Again, what you do in a relationship matters. Especially when food is involved.

Much like relationship advice, wherein everyone thinks they are an expert from lived experience, with the rise of Instagram and Yelp Elite status, everyone has become a "foodie." A provocateur of taste. A critic, a judge, a curator, and a tastemaker. A photographer and a copywriter. I mean, whatever happened to being just a gosh-darn happy eater? No. That is too plebeian.

Just for you, today only, for the low, low price of your attention for the remainder of this chapter, I have a special offer just for you. I have designed a proprietary matrix for you to determine what your food preferences say about your relationship. Hang on for the ride. And, you're welcome.

What to worry about regarding your relationship based on your food preferences:

Sushi

If you have to order nude food on a routine basis, how comfortable are you with being naked? Your relationship might suffer from a never-nude philosophy, where things are covered up and the lights are off. Delectable, though raw and uncooked, food is a metaphor for what you really want in your relationship and life: to be seen, discovered, and able to be your rawest self. Maybe slap some wasabi on yourself and feel something for once.

McDonald's

One of you hasn't grown up yet, and you are playing out your childhood fantasies with one another and with this meal. Your brand choice here hilariously speaks to the fact that you want to spend money and calories at an institution that used a clown to sell us fast food in the 1990s. Ask yourself: what unresolved issues from childhood are prompting me to order this happier meal? Better yet, ask your significant other. They'll love you for this deep, dark question when they're trying to just purchase their drive-through food in peace and quiet.

Happy Hour

While never paying retail speaks to my sense and sensibilities, you have to wonder why you're on a date getting slushy cocktails before 5:00 p.m. on the cheap. Does your date think you're cheap? Are you not worth the full-priced glass of merlot? Are you at a campy tiki cocktail bar throwing back slings of lime and lemon and lusciousness on the dime? If you are a routine happy hour goer, what does this say about your relationship? Is fun only allowed when it's discounted and at the senior hour of the day? Are you eating small bite plates at happy hour so your date does not have to buy you a full meal? Look, I'm all for saving money. I just think your dedication to the happiest hour must be scrutinized and analyzed for signs of cheapness. Cheap is not sexy. Being thrifty, because you want to go on a five-star vacation and buy a mansion is, however, something else entirely. We can discuss this over a half-priced glass of handcrafted Cabernet Sauvignon from a Bordeaux winery because this half-priced glass will be more expensive than most happy hours and taste twice as good. It's about value, folks.

Morton's The Steakhouse

The first time I wandered into a Morton's The Steakhouse, I was a college student who had never seen a Boston winter. I was mildly lost, since this was before cell-phone-enabled GPS would literally tell me what steps to take from door to door anywhere in the world. And this level of Siberian-style cold was a world away from my familiar Southern California. My dewy skin began to form icicles on my eyelids, and my sun-thinned blood required sustenance. I was ravenously hungry, and tremendously poor. I looked at the prix fixe menu and at my date who was equally impoverished, cold, and hungry, and together, we resembled under-dressed waifs out of a Charles Dickens novel. It was also Valentine's Day weekend, which is a scam for everyone who wants to travel during the President's Day holiday weekend. Oh, you thought I think it's a scam because of romance? No. I'm a romantic. Not a hopeless one. A hope-FULL one. Hope springs eternal, no matter how much life tries to beat it out of you. Anyway, if you go to a chain steakhouse, I think it says you don't know fine dining. This is acceptable at the age of nineteen, when a $130 dinner bill in February makes you think you might be poor all year. But if you plan a date out and about, and a $130 bill is no longer a source of multi-month destitution, please select a non-chain establishment. I'm not against franchises and chains, categorically speaking. But if you're unable to source a bespoke, dimly lit, fabulously smoky cocktail list to accompany your steak stuffed with Boursin cheese and topped with garlic butter and chives, and have a live jazz band playing in the background, then I'm not sure what the point is. Your sourcing of these experiences will speak to the future of your relationship happiness. Choose wisely.

Korean Highlight Tour: BBQ, Fried Chicken, Tofu Soup

If you think that Korean food consists simply of barbecue—that fabulously marinated meat with the perfect balance of sweet and salty, grilled to perfection right before your eyes—then you're missing out on the full experience. There's also double-fried chicken. Literally, the chicken is fried, rested, and fried again to golden, crispy perfection with a multiple layer crunch between you and the succulent flesh. Sorry, vegans. The sauce vehicle to this crispy paradise might spike your lips with a plump pepper taste, or you might enjoy the soy-garlic sauce, or even honey apple.

Importantly, Korean cuisine has what I like to call Seoul-Soul food, also known as tofu soup. This is the kind of multi-layered vegetable broth of carrots, radishes, napa cabbage, and onions that has been made with love from a grandma's recipe and is decorated with tender vegetables...fantastically fermented vegetables. The soon tofu is so soft and luscious it perfectly absorbs the umami fat flavor from the very thinly sliced beef now floating to the top of your soup for an easier bite of paradise. I cry over this soup. If you find that your relationship gravitates toward Korean cuisine, generally, I submit to you that you are probably longing for adventure—the kind of expansion of your soul when you awaken to new flavors, new textures, and new tastes, and discover an entirely new world. Is your relationship spaciousness enough to allow you to take flight with these ambitious adventures? Slurp your soup surreptitiously as you consider.

American Diner

Like any patriotic American, I love downhome griddle cooking. If you are the type of couple who seeks out diner food, which includes coffee burned to the bottom of the carafe, pancakes served all day (bless you, thank you for this sanity), eggs fried in grease from other meals, and burgers that are equally messy as they are simple, this suggests you are nostalgic for the way things used to be. And how did they used to be, I wonder? When was "back then" and how was it better than today? While grounding into traditional values is acceptable, I just wonder if you have accepted *you* now. Are you living in the now? Or are you living for a time that's passed? How comfortable are you creating a future relationship together if you're looking to the past as guidance? It's best to opine over existential questions with over-easy eggs, in my humble, eggcellent, self-sourced opinion.

California Fusion Cuisine

For everyone who isn't in California, let me quickly explain this. This is California at its finest. We take everything from everyone and spit it out as ours. That's why the entertainment industry has been built and thrived here. We are creative copycats. Labeling something as "California fusion cuisine" could mean, literally, anything. It probably leans toward healthy, less-processed foods, more from the farm than from the production facility kind of thing. Think about a lot of vegetables, a balanced amount of protein, some interesting ingredients you're not sure of how to pronounce, and a large wine menu because we grow such happy grapes here in this golden state. If your preference gravitates here, I would ask your relationship: are you longing to be more creative? Is there anything you do that stands out? Do you *want* to stand out? Why is it important to be seen? Do you have an ego issue or are you generally trying to connect with someone? In California especially, these are key questions in our image-driven culture. And California fusion cuisine might be being consumed because it's good for your relationship image. What's under the surface, y'all? This would be a good time to ask your date something really spooky like, "Tell me about the first time someone close to you died." How are you supposed to get to know someone if you don't know what they feel about the transition into the afterlife? Light cuisine paired with dark conversation. A new date idea!

Fish and Chips

One of my all-time favorite lunch dates was on the Venice Beach Boardwalk. We went to a fish and chips stand. It was sublimely simple. You only had to order one thing. If you take your date to a restaurant that only makes one thing, either you're a genius of simplicity or you're afraid of choices.

Let's take the positive example first: sometimes the nicest thing someone can do is prune options and make a decision. Wishy-washy is the absolute worst and should be reserved for a drive-through car wash only, not anywhere near dating. Unless your date loves you enough to wash your car for you. This is even better. Gentle people everywhere, please wash your significant other's car for them in a non-creepy way. "Hey, I need your keys so I can do something nice for you," is usually enough to get permission. Throw in an oil change? Gold. Trust me on this.

On the negative side of a simplified fish and chips experience, perhaps your date has no imagination. They only like one food, so they take you to the one place that serves the one meal that they like in exclusivity. It could happen.

In-N-Out Burger

In the spirit of equal opportunity, I judge my friends, family, and dates on their In-N-Out orders. I think it's a fascinating experiment. There's only a few things on the actual, literal menu. Then, you see, there's a whole secret menu. If you grew up in Southern California and have never bothered to learn the secret menu, I don't trust your investigative and conversational skills. In fact, I wonder if you have a probing imagination at all. And if you know the secret menu, and don't order off of it, well, that's just pure insanity because it has the best accoutrements available.

When someone offers me dessert or In-N-Out Animal Style fries off the secret menu, I take the latter all day, every day, any day of the week. If you roll through the drive-through together, ask your date about their biggest secrets. "Tell me something no one else knows about you," you would say while casually ordering your dreamy, secret menu fries. If their palms sweat or they have no secrets, this is not the good kind of fishy. Go fish. Find a new ocean, my friends.

Cheese and Charcuterie Board

There are multiple layers of assessment available here. Did your date craft a cheese and charcuterie board on your behalf? This would be an encouraging sign that they have artistic and creative tendencies. But more importantly, this shows they can plan and execute something of value. This tells me that your relationship is in a healthy place for future growth. If they have the plate catered, this is acceptable, although it receives less creativity points. Additionally, it could mean they would be the kind of person who would engage someone else to buy you a present on a special occasion rather than picking it out themselves. Which is fine if you're one of those people who just want something expensive. But just something to watch out for. It's my job to plant enough doubt that you have your eyes wide open. If they went to Trader Joe's or Whole Foods and sourced the ingredients and took you on a picnic, this is also heartening. It probably means they can go to the grocery store by themselves and choose an upscale, yuppy, crunchy store. (And hopefully you agree it's best to date adults who can feed themselves from the grocery store without your direct interference and assistance.)

Soup Dumps

Dim sum is a revelation. It's a soup, in a dumpling. Which means, there is hot, spicy, umami-infused liquid delivered straight to your mouth in a doughy bread vehicle. Think about a miniature bread bowl, with sausage encased in a delicious, riveting broth. And, look, it's about a billion degrees hot, too. I didn't know this when I took a bite of it right out of the steamer. The dumplings deceptively arrive, presumably ready to go, at the table in a steam basket, perky and available, and they don't have a sign that says, "Steaming hot bucket of liquid that will assuredly burn your tongue like no coffee ever has." I'm an enthusiast; the kind of person who dives head-on into deep and formative relationships, new cities, Super Bowl seven-layer dip, real estate flips, and dumplings. There is no waiting. I just go for it. I have never been in physical, literal, agonizing pain as much as when I burned my mouth for the first time on a soup dump.

If you are taken on a date to get soup dumps, first of all, don't call them this. It's gross. Second, if your date knows you are a pure life-enthusiast and never hesitate to dive head-in, and they don't bother to warn you that this new food you're about to ingest runs at the approximate temperature of the Sun, then you should dump them and keep the soup dumps.

In the type of relationship where one seeks out dumplings, you should wonder what your relationship is hiding. Dumplings are a vehicle to hide lots of delicious things. Depending on how the tables have turned, be the date that asks, "What types of things do you like to hide?" I know someone who hides their discarded junk food wrappers from their partner. After consumption, they hide the trash bag in another bag, and immediately deposit it to the larger, outdoor receptacle. Eating scalding hot food that is a literal metaphor for hidden and deep pockets gives you plenty of runway to explore what the deeper, hidden meaning might be behind your partner's behavior or proclivity to approach dangerously hot food with either suspicion or zest.

French Food

My favorite French restaurant in Los Angeles has been located in Echo Park since 1927. In Los Angeles, there is this freeway called the 405. The 405 is the central dividing line that will delineate your habits, style, friendships, wardrobe, and general aura of being. If you live west of the 405 freeway, you love brunch, rosé all day, low-key concerts, riding your bicycle between the Santa Monica Pier and the Venice Beach Boardwalk, likely work in technology, perhaps moved to California from the mid-Western flyover states, and own a small dog. If you live east of the 405 freeway, you have tattoos, dress enthusiastically from the thrift store, wear Birkenstocks, love craft coffee, listen to alternative rock music, eat the crust on your deep-dish pizza, and grow plants in your home. Different strokes for different folks. So, on the west side of town, you might find a bourgeois, upscale French restaurant. On the east side of town, you will find my favorite place: a dimly lit, ancient establishment with ruby red booths, antique smoky mirrors on the ceiling, French-blue wallpaper, and wait staff wearing tuxedos. It is a step back in time to another age, perhaps the age when the French 75 cocktail was first invented and gin was illegal during the Prohibition. Wait, yes, that's actually when this spot opened: 1927. The best thing to order is the trout almondine.

If you find that your relationship gravitates toward French cuisine, ask yourself: is it upscale or down-home? If you are lackluster in the romance department of your relationship, French food is rich fodder to woo your beloved. Buy them some roses before popping open the champagne. Stay after dinner and linger over your Beaujolais wine, and order the cheese plate instead of a sweet dessert. Determine if your relationship is as cosmopolitan and sophisticated as an artfully executed French 75 cocktail. If not, light things up brighter than the chandelier.

Breakfast Anytime

I'm not sure why establishments who fire up the griddle at any time of day don't realize that they should keep it on for all times of day. Breakfast served until 11:00 a.m. has to be one of the saddest signs I've ever read. It's a sign telling you that all your life choices have led you awry, you're lazy, overslept (again), probably have body odor and bad morning breath, and now you can't even enjoy pancakes. It's even more upsetting than a sign I just saw in my neighborhood, posted to a telephone poll, with a guy named "Dateable Jack" advertising himself for a date. His qualifications? Acceptable hygiene. What's "acceptable"? Do you floss for oral health or only floss as a dance move? I also really wonder why we have telephone poles up at all anymore. Do they conduct the Internet? If not, let's tear 'em out and plant some trees.

If you are lucky enough to be at a breakfast place and eat breakfast at any time of day with your date, your relationship is about making up your own rules as you go. Breakfast at 2:00 p.m.? No problem. Breakfast at 2:00 a.m.? No problem. You don't care. You fly in the face of convention. Tradition is for bucking. The only thing that concerns me here is if you aren't capable of developing a routine that works for you. Some of the best routines are those that are routine-less, naturally, like while on vacation. But if you are a person who is seeking out breakfast at 2:00 a.m. regularly, that's going to be a hard pass for me with a bedtime of 8:45 p.m. (My friends told me, "Thank you, Grandma," for staying out to have ice cream at 9:00 p.m. this past weekend.) Breakfast anytime is a metaphor for freedom, but I will take a pass at taking this literally. I've never awoken at the witching hour of 3:33 a.m. and said to myself, "Let's get flapjacks."

Ramen

Next to cocktails, soup must have some of the highest margins on planet Earth. Think about it. It's mostly water. You're paying to go outside of your home and slurp salted water with accessories. Good accessories. Umami accessories. But accessories, nonetheless, to a hot bowl of liquid. Want to sink your teeth into succulent, charred pork? Great. Here's a slice and a half. Paying extra to get Kobe beef barley seared? Okay, awesome. Here's just a half of a slice. It's pure portioned genius on the restaurant's part.

There are a few different types of ramen establishments. Ramen-ramen would be the kind of ramen you expect with luscious egg noodles, soy broth, vegetables, and a limited selection of bottled beer. Then, there's spicy ramen. This is my favorite place to take my friends who are from outside of the United States. Thoroughly, I like to get a rise out of people by introducing them to foods they have never tried. British people and spicy ramen is my favorite friend-food combo of late. The broth is so spicy that there is a numbing agent, so you can select your pepper spice level along with your numbing agent level, and turn your bowl of noodles into a science experiment with a heavy load of math. "Yes, I'd like to select the four-spice level with the five-numbing agent, please." When in doubt, numb it out.

Finally, there's dipping ramen. This requires the most dexterity as the noodles arrive to you, cold, and you must plunk them into the broth by using your chopsticks. Have you ever tried to move cold pasta around? It's slippery and feisty and somehow doesn't want to take a dive into the hot tub of decadent delight. At first, I would spill as many noodles on the counter as would land in my soup bowl, and this is before I could even get them near my mouth. With the pork broth being simmered for over thirteen hours, the issue is that the broth isn't as hot as I'd like it to be because the noodles are much colder than I'd like them to be. Temperature, much akin to life timing, matters here.

If you are the kind of couple who seeks out ramen experiences of all shapes and sizes of bowls and spice levels, you seem adventurous and cosmopolitan. If your coupledom cannot survive a conversation about the appropriate temperature of soup—there is a wrong answer and that's anything less than scalding—it's troubling to know how you could ever pull off creating a cozy temperature at home together. One day you're arguing about the temperature of your ramen. The next day you're arguing about the temperature of the bed and blaming those who sleep too hot. Then one person vacates the bed, and you're suddenly in a sexless relationship because of an unresolved debate about the proper temperature. These things could escape quicker than I can drop some cold ramen noodles on a countertop while attempting to deftly wield plastic chopsticks.

Chicken and Waffles

Similar to a fish-and-chips excursion, going to a restaurant that specializes in one thing is really a great way to simplify your life. Gone are the hours you could spend agonizing over the best thing to order on the menu prior to even stepping foot in the restaurant. The streamlined ordering options are simple. This eliminates stress and provides a happier, healthier life. And now that you've saved all those stress hormones to become a healthier, happier you, you can now splurge those calories on your chicken and waffles supreme special.

The best and only place to get chicken and waffles in Los Angeles is called Roscoe's House of Chicken 'N Waffles. I have been to the original one in Hollywood. I have been to the original one in Pasadena. I'm still confused as to which place is "original" as these two establishments are miles and miles apart from one another. I've never gotten a straight answer on which is the "real" original. The chicken, however, is exemplary at both. Imagine a fluffy (but not too fluffy) buttermilk waffle. It's low to the plate and is perfectly spacious enough for you to slather on real cow's milk, bonafied-cholesterol-rich melty butter. Next to this plate, you have buttermilk fried chicken done the down-home, Southern way with a hint of paprika and smokiness to perfectly compliment the waffle that has taken a bath in butter and a shower in syrup. Honestly, I would rather eat this meal in solitude and silence to leave room for the groans of pleasure that will ensue. It gets awkward when you have another person tagging along, sometimes.

If you go get chicken and waffles and your date has a question about the menu, this is a very bad sign. There's only one thing to order, and that's chicken and waffles. People who spend time debating over things like which cut of the chicken they want or if they want one waffle or two waffles sound like they're speaking in Dr. Seuss. A worse offense would be to go to a chicken and waffle house and order biscuits and gravy. Yes, this might be on the menu. But it's not why we're here. If this happens to you, you are probably out and about with a contrarian. If you are into that sort of thing—the kind of person who questions everything, everyone, and every move—well, cool. In my experience, they're asking a billion questions and behaving with an ego because they consider themselves enlightened. And that leaves me frightened. Any one person who pretends to know everything is not accepting the simple, sturdy, sane reality that no one knows anything. We're all making it up as we go. And thank goodness to the heavens that someone made up chicken and waffles. Bless you.

Smoothie Run

Speaking of running, is it true that couples who stay fit together will only see the cardiologist every other year after fifty? Asking for a friend, just so I know what to worry about in the upcoming decades. One of my favorite couples to babysit for when I was a teenager would go to a weekly community event in Santa Barbara called Nite Moves. This event involved a 1k ocean swim and a 5k run, after which you enjoyed a beer garden, live music, and appetizers. My job was to play in the sand with the kids while the parents went off and lived their *Baywatch* fitness dreams together. I wanted to be just like them when I grew up. And yet, here I am, writing this book: not a housewife with five children, not married to a doctor who likes to go jogging with me just for fun. Some people have it all, and others drink fine wine and eat Cheez-Its in bed while crying into their bathrobe to muffle the sounds of sorrow.

If your date wants to take you on a smoothie run, this is a positive sign they care about your longevity and overall well-being. Eating plants and letting medicine be thy food is nice until it becomes dogma. Then, you might find yourself suddenly with a vegan who wants you to become vegan, too. And you lose a good eighteen months of your life to eat plant-based because your partner said they'd rather die than be with someone who eats meat. Again, when it comes to "'till death do us part" or divorce court, the latter is less expensive and doesn't require an autopsy. Divorce, after all, is simply getting sued. So, I guess what I'm saying is, smoothie runs can turn into vegan dogma debacles, which eventually could land you in divorce court. Sip carefully.

Tapas

Small plates full of sumptuous food could never be a wrong decision. I decided not to become friends with a girl, once, who said she categorically hates Spanish food and specifically hates tapas. Unthinkable. I can't get down with that. No, we cannot be friends. I'm not even sorry for drawing this boundary. Who could refuse olives, cheese, ham, vegetable crudités, spreads, sauces, and buttered bread? It's some of the best food on the planet. Paired with a Tempranillo wine or a dry, sparkling Cava and this might be my favorite date food thus far. Even better if we're in Spain and we just ride horses bareback on the beach. I guess you can't have it all. But you can have all the food, and that counts for something. If your date does not appreciate the romance and shareability of small-plated delicacies, I'm not sure that they are as interested in romance as you might be. If you think it's not a romantic gesture for me to let you have the last slice of the Manchego cheese, then you can't appreciate the kind of sharing I have to give.

The Wurst Sausage

Rolling up to a hipster sausage counter housing exotic blends of pheasant, alligator, duck, and the like makes me feel that my pedestrian love of chicken and jalapeno sausage is blasé. I have the worst time at the wurst shop, pun intended. The wannabe foodie in me craves the ability to tell my coworkers about trying alligators. I mean, talk about a different kind of *tailgate* party. But the sensible, safe me, wants to be cozy and comfortable with a choice I've made over and over again. If you find yourself on a date at a sausage place, ask yourself if this is too overt. There's no metaphor or mystery involved in the relationship anymore if you've been taken to a wurst haus. Next they'll likely ask you, "How do you like your meat?"

Vegan Thai Food

"I just love tofu," said no one ever. Tofu, like mayonnaise, is not something you go around saying you like. However, tofu does pass the fried test: a scientific experiment wherein you determine if something is better as it was intended, or fried. The latter is almost unequivocally true. And this process might require deep research.

If you go to a specifically vegan Thai food restaurant, this exhibits an extreme lack of creativity. Almost any traditional Thai food restaurant serves tofu, steamed (gross) or fried (glorious). And if you bother to go all the way out of your way to go to a vegan place, this tells me that your politics really *do* affect the way you live. And kudos to you. But I can't stand egg rolls that don't have pork in them, so I'll pass.

Kabob

How do you like your steak cooked? *Medium.* The objectively best temperature at which to order a piece of red meat is *medium*. What a sad description. What's interesting about this meat? It's medium. How do you like it done? Medium. The word itself, not the meat, is tepid and does not tantalize. I think medium meat should just be called "well done." Because I want it done well. Well done, on the other hand, means you've killed the meat, killed my joy, and killed the meal. It's the fastest way to ruin a good food time, hands down, bar none. Nothing has been more misleading than a well done piece of filet mignon. Here's a couple of good rules to live by: 1) once the meat turns gray, it's likely time to go home, and 2) when you look like your passport photo, it's definitely time to go home.

I consider it a lifetime achievement award that I have eaten so much food. I could switch now to smoothies for the rest of my lived-out days and probably be just fine. But from this food, I have actually experienced life. Or something like life. Something also like heartburn, indigestion, massive weight gain, a burned mouth, and a bankrupt bank account. There was also the elation of experience, an introduction to interesting cultures, and new, fascinating, stimulating, glorious taste.

And if you find yourself in a relationship lacking physical intimacy, the thing about food is that it doesn't ask for much in return for you to accept its pleasure. It's there for you, night or day, day or night to give you its delight. So, if your love life lacks passion and the fire of desire, there's a chicken wing that will singe your ever-loving lips off with its heat, or a bowl of ramen that will literally numb the entirety of your mouth with a ghost pepper. If you can't feel everything you want to feel, sometimes it's enough to know you can still feel something. I have dug deep and gone the mouth-watering and life-altering distance for the research of this book.

Perhaps you and your dear one, your twin flame, soul mate, lover and friend are able to laugh about this chapter while the TV is on in the background and you're arguing over which cuisine to order in. Or, you're an adorably fit health-nut couple who roasts veggies and grills chicken while a good night in for you includes candlelit yoga. Or, you're together with someone but feel distant as the relationship is different and changed as much as you are now, too.

Like water, relationships can move glacially slow or waterfall fast. The rain sometimes pelts as much as it is a misty sheen at other moments. The latter of which is what brings the rainbow.

Perhaps you find yourself single, and wanting to mingle. Or, single and not ready to mingle. Single comes with a lot of assumptions, the least true of which is that being single means you're alone. Single can be good. Single can be as such that ordering sushi for one feels like just enough fun. Not too much fun, only the right amount. Because now, you don't have to share the baked white fish Godzilla roll that you'd always rather eat all to your selfish self, anyway. Oops, maybe that's just me.

And what is love if not occasionally lost, without ever being found? After all is said and done, and the lights have turned down low, and you find yourself wanting to dance real slow...sometimes the only reasonable thing to do and place to go is out to eat. Alone.

The strangest thing about dining alone is knowing where to look and what to do with your hands. The second piece is remedied easily with a stemmed wine glass. You have something to play with, to twirl. But where to look when you're alone? That's a harder one. I love eavesdropping, so that's a good sport. I love looking at couples and wondering if they're actually in love, pretending to be in love, on pause but might resume being in love, are passionately friends who were never really in love... I keep making up endings. Or maybe beginnings. This sport has some drawbacks. If you peer into someone's soul long enough to try to understand them, they might notice you staring. And that's just awkward. So, I'm still learning what to do with my eyes. I don't want to look down, looking down is sad. If there is a view, you can easily cast your gaze on the horizon. Now when I look pensive, it's not threatening.

I have a few rules for going out to eat alone:

Elegant and Expensive

My preference for eating out is somewhere exotic, expensive, and elegant. A sublime place with a fantastic food flight that exceeds my own culinary skills. More easily put, this rule states: *do not select cuisine you could easily craft at home.* While dining out alone, I would prefer crisp linens, warm candles, dangling chandeliers, and a wine pairing menu that reads like a novel. Who are we kidding? I'd like this dining out anywhere, with anyone, too.

Dress Up

Sweat suits are for the hiking trail. A solo date calls for an adorable outfit. Not because someone will see you, but expressly because *you* will see you. That's enough of a reason. Do your hair. Do your makeup. Listen to the type of music that gets you pumped up. Pre-game with champagne at home. Go all in.

Shoulders Down and Back

This is no time for slumping. Puff the chest. Stand up straight. Confront solo dining with dignity, grace, and fantastic posture. The only way to face singledom is full-frontal confrontation with exemplary posture.

Remove the Extra Place Setting

Once seated at the restaurant, kindly ask the friendly waitstaff to remove the extra place setting. This way, everyone knows that you're not waiting for someone else. It's the best way to avoid those pesky questions like, "Are you waiting for another guest?"

Slow Down

Despite the fact that you'll be conversing with three people—me, myself, and I—it's natural there might be long lulls and some uncomfortable silences. Don't rush through the meal. Savor the experience. Taste the actual flavors.

Never Accept Pity

Others might send pitying glances to you. But never, ever pity yourself. Never give up, never surrender. Don't be sad. Have another glass of wine if you need to, just get home safely.

While normally I believe everyone is too self-absorbed and addicted to their phone screens to notice anything I am doing, I have found that dining out alone does create a bit of a scene. People look at me, wondering why. When I was in Madrid, Spain, I knew just enough Spanish to realize what the wait staff were saying behind my (literal) back, i.e., asking how someone could simultaneously be attractive and alone. Other times, I have had nicely meaning people ask me, "How could someone like YOU be out ALONE?" Wow. What confidence these strangers have on my behalf; and what wondrous, unsolicited feedback I tend to receive on my solo dining dates. These things just are the way they are, sometimes. Most of the time I get compassionate glances from older women dining in companionable silence with their mates. The longer the couple has been together, it seems, the less they speak to each other over a meal out. I feel cheered on by the general public by just existing. Or else, I have an ego problem.

I have had many female friends tell me it's incredibly brave to dine alone. I don't think that I'm being a particularly fierce brand of CourageousCass™ when I am simply eating crepes, double-fisting a mimosa and cappuccino simultaneously, and of course having my nose stuffed in a book (where else)? On a solo dining adventure, I often get sent a free drink from the kitchen, a free glass of wine or champagne, a free latte, or a free something-or-other. I don't know why. I'm simply slowing down, being kind, and making sure in no uncertain terms to wait to live my life until I have "arrived" somewhere else. Here is all I have. Here is all I know. Here is home, even for a free spirit like me.

Any meal, I've learned, can be your last. So make these meals, come as they may, decadent, delectable, and decidedly memorable. The last exquisite meal I enjoyed all in my own company was in London, England. Previously, I had elected to make 2020 the year to be authentically me, no matter what the cost. And hence, I had given notice on a life that took the oxygen out of my soul, which meant leaving a city, a job, and a relationship all within the span of a couple weeks. The scene of this final meal, as it came to be, was in March 2020, right before the world shut down for COVID-19.

I was temporarily living in London and thought it could be my home. Pretending to be a local, and determined to soak up the arts and culture, I had just visited the Royal Academy of Arts to see an expansive exhibition of Picasso, one of my favorites. The exhibit left me in literal tears. Yes, I take myself on lovely dates—alone—because the company and conversation are so rich and warm it's hard to imagine another person getting a word in edgewise.

I sashayed over to Fortnum & Mason. When I'm walking alone, I'm usually half-dancing, just the kind of motion that keeps people guessing what I'd do next if they were not looking at their phone. I've realized you can get away with almost anything nowadays because no one sees you. I literally danced my way all around London, occasionally breaking into a full, theatrical song and dance, and literally no one noticed. Anyway, Fortnum & Mason is a Neiman Marcus-type store filled with many floors of terrific trinkets and beautiful bobbits and very few humans foot-trafficking or buying things. I had no reservation for high tea, but I got a seat, anyway.

I waited for my table in a robin egg blue and gold-gilded foyer. There was a man playing show tunes and popular songs on the piano. The chandeliers were lit up, even though it was the middle of the day, outside was still gray and glistening with leftover raindrops. I was shown to my table, and dined alone next to another woman who was also dining alone. She was American. I could tell she didn't want to be friendly, so I did not strike up a conversation. This time *I* was the warm smile greeting her and silently cheering her on. She looked local, and this was inspiring.

I ordered the savory tea selection with champagne. I was told I could have unlimited refills on everything. This was the classy version, my friends, of a Las Vegas buffet. Because in this scenario, they brought everything to me on a literal silver platter. (When that particular metaphor becomes mundane, put me out to pasture.)

Of all the things I got to try, the standout feature was lobster eggs. This was The Queen Mother's favorite dish, according to the waiter. Imagine an egg salad with chunks of rich lobster meat curiously folded in. The texture is almost like mousse. It is served in a hollowed-out egg with a tiny spoon meant for someone even smaller than me, which is hard to imagine as I never held a spoon that made me look larger than life. When I asked for another lobster egg, I received three. A Holy Trinity. Bottoms up.

As my tea was poured, my champagne refilled, and an ungodly portion of lobster eggs sat in front of me, I was informed that the borders of the United Kingdom would be closing soon and it would be prudent to return to the United States of America. I had the most distinctly un-British reaction...i.e., there was no keeping calm to carry on. I cried. Publicly. I was like a cartoon character; tears were being thrown out of my tear ducts in horizontal fits. Tears were not spilling down my cheeks, they were literally flinging themselves out of my eyes violently, fast, and without warning. I barged into the water closet, and sobbed into a fancy hand towel. Thank goodness for a meltdown at the kind of place that has cloth napkins. Good gracious.

I would like to say that I composed myself and finished my elegant meal in an equally elegant fashion. No. I blabbed and blubbered and breathed through my tears. Suddenly, cake arrived. I hadn't ordered cake. This happens to me a lot. Maybe it's why I had such weight to shed—it was all the free extras I got from dining alone.

At that moment, I realized, there was no food that could fill my aching heart. Not lobster eggs. Not champagne. Not cake. Nothing luxurious and lovely could make me feel any less lonely and utterly wretched.

Sometimes you fall in love with a person. Sometimes you fall in love with a book. Sometimes you fall in love with a city. Sometimes you fall in love with a food dish. Sometimes you fall in love with a poem. Sometimes you fall in love with a piece of art that moves your very soul. Sometimes you fall in love with a wish, a dream, a hope. The last is the trickiest because it is the most elusive. Ever moving. Never pinned down. Never fleshy and focused, it remains on the hopeful horizon, ever out of reach.

Thousands of miles from home, without a real, proper rain jacket, I was caught in London in an in-between and fragile life. I had moved abroad to finally live out all my hopes and dreams, and it only lasted a matter of weeks. I was heartbroken to leave London, but more importantly I was heartbroken to have felt I was finally living my fullest life dreams before I had to switch gears and find a new dream. It was out of my control. I was out of my scope as an A-type personality contingency planning for contingency planning.

I have loved.

I have lost.

I have been loved.

And I felt incredibly lost.

I thought that if I lost my taste for life, I would never lose my taste for good food. I was wrong. I thought that if I was far from home, food and food alone would bring me a sense of comfort. I was wrong. I thought if love could let you down, food never would. And I was wrong.

I worried that if love let me down, food would be there. And it was.

But food wasn't what I needed.

What I needed was a full spirit. A full life. So that's what I'm up to now—living. Fully, really, *actually* living.

And you know what?

I'm less worried now. Because in the threadbare moments of my life, I took the broken and busted strings and learned how to weave a new tapestry. I rewrote the story of shame, of not-enough-ness, and of failure. I took the messy moments and learned to create a masterpiece. Not one for the world to look at, but one that I could see in the reflection of the mirror and say, "I love you, Cassie." And mean it, this time.

Wherever you are and whatever food you have tried to use to stuff into the hole of your heartbreak—love lost, travel plans lost, home lost, people lost, jobs lost, creativity lost, pets lost, intimacy lost, friends lost, your past self lost—I believe you can also transform your pain. You can find hope. Hopefully you know that, too.

    Romantic love wasn't all I needed.

    Food wasn't all I needed.

    Life is all I need.

    And the purpose of life? It's simply this: to live it.

Chapter 12

Let's Worry about Happy-ish

"Has anyone by fussing in front of the mirror ever gotten taller by so much as an inch?"
—Matthew 6:27

Growing up, one of my most arduous wishes was to be taller than my mom. Specifically, I wanted to be 5'3" tall. I knew well enough that a wish and prayer alone wouldn't buy me much height. I needed a tactical plan. So, I held off from drinking coffee until I was seventeen, stretched my spine diligently, and ate a lot of green vegetables. I hit just over 50% of the goal. I am taller than my mama, but I'm only 5'2.5". There's nothing like setting a goal in life of which you, quite literally, cannot control the outcome. And thus, I have perpetually suffered from the idea that I will be short forever. Much like the second law of thermodynamics and the world marching toward entropy, I imagine I will only get shorter and shorter over time. This is why I spent a lot of time on the bed or floor lying like a cadaver and stretching my spine, which some people call yoga, in an attempt to elongate and promote a healthy shelf life for the little height I managed to achieve.

Life is like that sometimes. Sometimes you get what you want. Sometimes you stay low to the ground forever, and ankle pants in a normal person's size will fit your petite frame without having to pay to get them tailored (this is one of my best life hacks, by the way).

I do wonder what worry has added to my life. Has it made it better? Has it made it worse? Who's the judge?

Let me give you a brief list of what *worry* has done for me:

Fit Right In

I come from an illustrious line of warriors. My Irish Great-Grandma Anne was affectionately known as Anxious Annie. Because I knew her as a young child, I didn't have the distinct pleasure of co-worrying with her. But I love the heritage of histrionics, here. Generally speaking, people *do* worry. About *things*—about everything, about *anything*—especially if you're in my company. And I realized that worrying is a bit like oxygen to a fire. The more you worry, the more things there are to worry about.

Vocalizing about worries doesn't always make it worse, nor better, it just usually adds a few more things to worry about. It's kind of like science: worry multiplied by new things to worry about has a transmutative property to produce additional items for discussion, debate, delineation, and eventually more worry. Simply put: worry begets worry, which begets worry—and the world turns on its axis to the tune of our collective "Oy vey!"

Kept Me Outta Crime

Look, I could be a con artist. Or a gambler. Or an alcoholic. Or an international arms dealer. But I'm not. I'm just a plain old, no-frills, down to earth (most days) worrywart. Or more nicely put: a fussbudget. So I like to justify my bad habits at times by saying, "It could be worse." Then, I often go down a trail of how it *could* be worse and how if I *did* engage in an international life of crime, what kinds of arms dealer I would be and how I would ship crates of guns internationally. And this turns into a worry landscape, possibly turning into a future novel noir I have yet to write. The point is, worry is distasteful but it's not that bad. It could be worse. I could be addicted to reality television.

Cocktail Conversation

In polite company, apparently, you're not supposed to talk about sex, politics, and religion. But if I have a glass of alcohol in my hand and new people to meet, you'd better believe those are really the only things I care to know about strangers. I ask really easy, softball get-to-know you questions like, "Do you think the peaceful transfer of power will remain through the next election season?" or, "What role does metanarrative play in our postmodern society?" or, "Scale of 1-10: how comfortable are you in your own skin and why?" or, "When was the last time you considered death, both your own and as an eventual reality for everyone you know and love?" Because I generally have so many things to worry about and so much to learn about what *other* people worry about, this has given me endless cocktail conversation topics. Sometimes, I even get invited back for a full dinner party.

Found My Voice

If I'm being *really* honest—and I suppose I should be, now that we've spent so much time together—worrying has helped me find my voice. When I started speaking (literally and out loud) about the things that worried me, I broke out of the prison of my mind. That prison told me something like, "You're the only person who thinks about things too much, and has real concerns about the state of the world, the state of the universe, the state of being, the state of metaphysical inquiry, etc." The more *real* I got with my own thoughts, and started to vocalize them and observe them, the less they imprisoned me. Now I just stick to the occasional prison workout to stay fit and trim, and simulate a breakout every now and again.

Worrying hasn't made me literally taller. It hasn't made me (that much of) a worse human. It hasn't made me the world's best conversationalist, although I'm trying. But behind the worry, was a voice I needed to listen to...and that was my own.

I quickly realized that shooting for happiness is a bit worrisome. So before I even started writing a manuscript, I backed my goal down from happiness to *happy-ish*. *Happy-ish* seems like a target

I could hit, and so could you. It seems like something we could really, really do.

What is *happy-ish*?

I can answer it esoterically, but that might bore you and also put me to sleep. Then I wouldn't be able to finish the manuscript and you'd be left hanging.

Here's what *happy-ish* is to me now, in no particular order:

Nestling under an oak tree with branches spread out wide; the tree welcomes me in, gives me shade, allows me to sit and feel its roots, and thus feel my own.

Dancing on the beach alone and feeling the cold sand wiggle in between my toes as my hips sway to the rhythm of the crashing waves, and I feel connected with the tides and the oneness of all.

Bathing under the moon, wrapped up in a blanket and knowing my body is full of water, and it is moving with the moon tides just like the ocean. Remembering, in this moment, the very essence of nature and creation pulses with me.

Cooking luscious, nutritious green lentil pasta tossed with kale, arugula, Manchego cheese, and pesto finished with a perfectly poached egg on top.

Baking easy, one-bowl raspberry lemon mint muffins with mint grown in the garden right outside the kitchen window.

Learning a new language as the words tumble off my tongue in new and interesting ways, and feeling the sensation of describing something familiar with foreign words.

Ambling, sometimes aimlessly and almost every day, by the cemetery where my grandparents and great-grandparents are buried; feeling into the circle of life that beats with my very cells, alive with stories still to be written.

Conversing in a winding, wonderful way with friends new and old to hear stories never-been-told.

Writing poetry and weaving words in a way that creates a sense of play.

Witnessing my own expansion, and giving thanks for where I have been and where I am going, even though it's forward into the great unknown.

Coming home.

No matter how far you have wandered or how deeply you have worried, it is my wish that you can feel the fullness of who you really are. That the mystery and magic of this explosive, exciting, exuberant life will once again woo you with delight. And that you can fully, without abandon, bask in love and light.

I hope you find your happily ever after, and at minimum, your very own sense of happy-ish. Cheers, to you.

Life After Worry?

I have a recurring daydream that I'll find a life with no more worries. Maybe I will get whisked away, finally, to that retirement pineapple farm in Hawaii. Once in paradise, all my worries would have melted away, although hopefully not from the fiery volcano overhead. I would stick my toes in the sand, and hopefully not walk over a stingray as I'm sauntering along the beach. I would pursue swimming in the ocean daily, and hopefully not get eaten by a shark.

See, the thing is, even if I quit my life and went to live in paradise, my worries would follow me. I'd find something new to worry about. I just seem to have a gift to imagine, in great detail, what could go wrong.

I have self-judged, self-criticized, and self-analyzed this hyper-vigilant worry behavior from many angles. I have enlisted therapists, coaches, and trainers to help reduce, redefine, or rewire the worry. Recently, my doctor even offered to give me a genetic test to see if I worry more than the average person, but I declined because I told her I *know* I do. I'm not sure I need to pay a worrisome sum of money for a genetic test to tell me that medically speaking, I'm a worrier.

For the majority of my twenties, I played the "if only" game with my worries. If only I had the right job, I wouldn't worry. If only I lived in the right house, I wouldn't worry. If only I married the right person, I wouldn't worry. If only I could travel to Europe once a year, I wouldn't worry. If only I met new friends, I wouldn't worry. *If only...*

Later, I thought, for a moment, that I would outgrow my worry. Similar to my childhood allergies, maybe one day my worries would dissipate and disappear. Maybe I'd age out of worrying so much? As I crossed into my thirties, I felt I was getting older. Not just metaphorically. In my early twenties, I ran three half marathons in one year. I decided to run a half marathon again, at thirty-three, and let me tell you: the muscles, joints, bones, and tendons all have something to say when you take a decade off from long-distance running and decide to pick it up again. You start to wake up with new aches and pains in places you've never thought of before. Getting out of bed is just a little slower. And I'm supposed to be in the prime of my life!

Here I am... And, I still worry about things. I've worried about everything, and that is an ever-expanding topic.

So, let me shortcut the learnings of a lifelong relationship with worry: your worries will likely never completely evaporate or erase themselves from your life. A slight reframe is that worry is what tugs on my heart. It is what (comically) reminds me I'm alive, that I feel things, and I have hopes and dreams. Now when I worry, I ask my heart: can I listen to you deeper? Is there something that you want to tell me? Or am I just getting in my own head too much, and need to go play outside? (Thanks, Mom, for reminding me, still.)

I've learned to let worry become a side character—worry cannot play the protagonist or the producer. Worry can't call the shots. If we're going on a road trip, worry has to sit in the passenger seat. It can't drive. I won't let it.

Finally, I learned that by befriending my creativity, I could release my worries and actually live a life that felt impactful, exciting, and true to me. Through activating my creative center, I moved from a consumer of information to a creator of my own story. When I was able to turn on my creative flow, I was able to lose 50 lbs., design a new career, and write my first book (hey, that's how we became friends!). My worries never completely resolved, and I've picked up new ones along the way, but I've learned to work with my worry as an ally and achieve my dreams, anyway.

I hope my story inspires you to kick "worry" out of the driver's seat of your life, and let it come along for the ride as a passenger instead. Where you're going matters. Your dreams matter. The life you want to create matters. Just don't let worry get the last word. Be the main character in your life, don't ever give that slot away. No one can play you...like you.

Worry has been my constant companion and friend ever since I can remember. I can't actually remember a time in my life where I didn't worry... Instead of fighting it, I finally found a way to work with worry as an ally. To befriend worry instead of berating myself for worrying was a turning point that led me into a fuller, happier, more connected life—both with myself and with the world around me.

How'd I get there?

I started by writing a letter to "worry" and setting up a different relationship. Here is an excerpt from that letter:

Dear *worry*:

You've taught me a lot of things. What stands out is that you've always been there to warn me about what *could* go wrong. By calling out what could be dangerous, you have kept me safe. I haven't ever had a scrape I couldn't get out of, and I credit you with keeping me on my toes. Showing me possible negative consequences has kept me risk-averse by avoiding thinking too big or acting too bold.

You've been present, consistent, and caring in your own way. I have never needed to ask where you went, as you were right there all along. As a presence in my life, you have been relentless in your pursuit of closeness and constant communication.

Whenever I get lost listening to you, I have forgotten to check in with myself or ask for help from other people around me. We've had a very close relationship, sometimes at the exclusion of others. You have been a more constant companion to me than anyone else in my life.

We've seen quite a few milestones together. You've been there when I have felt successful to say, "*It won't last.*" And, you've been there when I felt like I failed to say, "*I told you so.*" No matter what I do or achieve, your sneaky message that I'm not enough has been branded onto my brain.

I know that your goal has been to help me survive.
But, now I want more. I want to *thrive*.

I will still need your help from time to time, only when there's a real emergency. You're welcome to pop in and say hello occasionally when something really big is happening that might cause me literal, actual harm. Until then, I'm sending you on a permanent vacation. I think you'll find a nice reprieve is well-timed. You've been on 24/7 duty now for my whole life. Aren't we both ready to shake things up and make a change?

I have become the person who can listen to my intuition, my intellect, and my instincts. Without you whispering in my ear constantly, I can actually take time to hear the wisdom of my body and soul.

As I graduate away from this close relationship with you, I want you to know I won't mess up or miss something important. I have a great community around me. Despite the fact that you have been my closest companion, I've learned to make other friends lately. I've been reaching out to people who love me and asking for help. It's been really good for me to branch beyond this dramatic duo of me and you.

It's easier to play small and stay safe when I listen to you. Now, I'm willing to take another path. Interested in what comes next, I am staying grounded in the present while expanding my excitement to explore a bigger, brighter, bolder future.

As I have given you permission to go on a permanent vacation, I am giving myself permission to go into permanent *living mode*. Fully living my own life, on my terms, with my luminous light turned on from the inside out. Shifting into a feeling of flow, I am willing to breathe easier, stand taller, speak truer, see clearer, hear fuller, and engage the world around me with honesty, humor, heart, and hope.

I don't know much about changing the world. I've just learned I can change myself. And I can change this relationship with you, worry, for the better, by saying a fond goodbye.

It's been real. Now, I need to get on to living my real life.

With gracious gratitude and abundant appreciation,
Cassie

If you'd like to write your own letter to "worry," start by being honest with yourself. You never need to show anyone else this letter. Sometimes, the words we most need to hear are the ones we tell ourselves.

Unleashing and unlocking your creativity is your greatest asset when it comes to setting up a life where worry doesn't control you. Activating my creative center is what freed me. It can free you, too.

To begin, shift into a neutral observer perspective. Don't judge what you write...just start writing.

Ready to break up with your worries?
My mission is to help people worry less and live fearlessly.

I help people change worry into curiosity to design a freer, happier life.
Interested in rewriting your relationship with worry, forever?
Let's chat at cassieshea.com.

Backword

"This book is a joke."

—Dan Shea
(Cassie's dad)

Resources

Still worried? It's okay. We've all been there. I got you!

My language of love is recommending books. So...here you go:

Stop Worrying about Money:
- *Money is Emotional: Prevent Your Heart from Hijacking Your Wallet* by Christine Luken
- *The Energy of Money* by Maria Nemeth
- *The Game of Life and How to Play It* by Florence Scovel Shinn
- *The Soul of Money* by Lynne Twist and Teresa Barker
- *Your Money or Your Life* by Joseph R. Domniguez and Vicki Robin

Stop Worrying about Relationships:
- *Anam Cara: A Book of Celtic Wisdom* by John O'Donohue
- *Conscious Loving: The Journey to Co-Commitment* by Gay and Kathlyn Hendricks
- *How to Be an Adult in Love* by David Richo
- *The Queen's Code* by Alison A. Armstrong
- *The Vortex* by Esther and Jerry Hicks
- *You Can Heal Your Heart* by Louise Hay and David Kessler

Stop Worrying about Your Career:
- *Conscious Living* by Gay Hendricks
- *Conscious Luck* by Gay Hendricks with Carol Kline
- *How Will You Measure Your Life?* by Clayton Christensen
- *Linchpin: Are You Indispensable?* by Seth Godin
- *Playing Big: Practical Wisdom for Women Who Want to Speak Up, Create, and Lead* by Tara Mohr
- *Sun Tzu and the Art of Business: Six Strategic Principles for Managers* by Mark R. McNeilly
- *The Art of Work* by Jeff Goins
- *The Happiness Track: How to Apply the Science of Happiness to Accelerate Your Success* by Emma Seppala
- *The Seven Spiritual Laws of Success* by Deepak Chopra
- *The Surrender Experiment* by Michael Alan Singer

Stop Worrying about How to Get Things Done:

- *Get It Done: From Procrastination to Creative Genius in 15 Minutes a Day* by Sam Bennet
- *Getting Things Done: The Art of Stress-Free Productivity* by David Allen
- *How to Begin: Start Doing Something That Matters* by Michael Bungay Stanier
- *Year of Yes: How to Dance It Out, Stand in the Sun and Be Your Own Person* by Shonda Rhimes

Stop Worrying about Your Well-Being:

- *A Course in Weight Loss* by Marianne Williamson
- *Becoming Supernatural* by Joe Dispenza
- *Energetic Boundaries* by Cyndi Dale
- *Loving What Is* by Byron Katie
- *The Emotion Code* by Bradley Nelson
- *The Power of Now* by Eckhart Tolle
- *The Seat of the Soul* by Gary Zukav
- *You Can Heal Your Life* by Louise Hay

Stop Worrying about Your Creativity (or Lack Thereof):

- *Big Magic: Creative Living Beyond Fear* by Elizabeth Gilbert
- *Real Artists Don't Starve* by Jeff Goins
- *The Artist's Way* by Julia Cameron
- *The War of Art: Break Through the Blocks and Win Your Inner Creative Battles* by Steven Pressfield

About Cassie

Cassie Shea is a short gal with a tall personality. Having lived in metropolitan cities such as Los Angeles and London, she loves culture, art, and music...but her real passion is reading and eating. Mac and cheese is still her favorite comfort food. A third-generation local from Santa Barbara, California, she loves the beach and can most often be found stand up paddle boarding, biking, hiking, perfecting the world's best one-bowl muffin recipe, or (nicely) pestering everyone she meets with endless questions to feed her insatiable curiosity. Want more lasting change and deeper insights in your own "life after worry"? Visit cassieshea.com to learn more about Cassie and her coaching practice.